# MGTOW

## BUILDING WEALTH AND POWER

# MGTOW

## BUILDING WEALTH AND POWER

### FOR SINGLE MEN ONLY

## TIM PATTEN

iUniverse®

# MGTOW BUILDING WEALTH AND POWER
## FOR SINGLE MEN ONLY

*In any gender studies endeavor we all must realize people are individuals and not all men are exactly alike men referenced within and not all women are all alike the women referenced within.*

*Characters in this book are actual people in real relationship situations. Names and places have been changed.*

*Cover Art: © Ardee Arollado, James Fickling,
Male Model: K Andrew Stiles*

*iUniverse books may be ordered through booksellers or by contacting:*

*iUniverse
1663 Liberty Drive
Bloomington, IN 47403
www.iuniverse.com
1-800-Authors (1-800-288-4677)*

*ISBN: 978-1-4917-8720-5 (sc)
ISBN: 978-1-4917-8721-2 (e)*

*Library of Congress Control Number: 2016900424*

*Print information available on the last page.*

*iUniverse rev. date: 01/05/2016*

# CONTENTS

# INTRODUCTION

*MGTOW, Building Wealth and Power* is both a celebration of modern masculinity and a practical guide to ensuring that men like us experience long-term contentment and have a better financial future. Inside this book are investing techniques that work; paying homage to the massive social movement of men which is ending entanglements and enhancing happiness through bachelorhood. This book features empowering insights on patriarchy, power, masculinity and the ancient secrets of creativity, as well as practical strategies for managing our money and building wealth. Also included are two campfire tales--for our ears only--that offer lessons on reorienting ourselves towards a more productive and enlightened existence.

Men are the most remarkable and innovative beings on Earth. We have harnessed every aspect of our world, from controlling fire to landing a space probe on a live comet. It is the author's hope that this book inspires you to draw on this innate power and help yourselves to live a better life. There's no doubt that each of us can tackle the goals we've dreamed of and longed for, but this is hard to achieve without taking certain steps. Throughout history, having sufficient resources--money--has allowed men to be free and powerful. Inside is encouragement for all of you to budget, save and invest.

# CHAPTER 1

# What is MGTOW?

Men Going Their Own Way (MGTOW) is a fast growing, worldwide phenomenon based on a philosophy which can be used by a man for gaining control over his own personal freedom and future. It has been referred to as the modern men's liberation movement, delivering men as a gender from subjugation. MGTOW is a lifestyle that frees men from patriarchal traditions regarding expectations for dating, living entanglements and marriage. It liberates men from a life of tiresome labor, waste of personal resources and costly emotional exhaustion often devoted to toxic mates, girlfriends or wives.

## The Red Pill

MGTOW is sometimes referred to as "Taking the Red Pill." Just as in *The Matrix*, the Red Pill enables those who swallow it to see the surprising reality behind conventional living together and the false ideology of marriage. Feminism teaches people to develop a critical lens when looking at the world and the roles and tasks involved in any life and routine. Then people can see domination and oppression. It requires effort. This is exactly what men are doing when they take the Red Pill. MGTOW is opening the eyes of ordinary men to a fresh perspective, a clarity. Men will realize new possibilities after seeing the painful truth that men have been compliant with a hierarchical social order that imposes abusive expectations and directives upon them.

## Global Awareness of Gynocentric Domination

MGTOW[iii] is an increasing global awareness paradigm that helps men avoid dangerous relationships within a Gynocentric society. For the purpose of this book, Gynocentric society means one which exalts women's physical, financial and emotional needs over all others.[i] MGTOW views the world through a critical Gynocentric lens, or focusing your binoculars just as college level gender studies teaches. Oftentimes, individuals discover the MGTOW message after a conventional relationship turns poisonous and causes them anger or deep pain.

## Some, but not all, MGTOW men ascribe to these ideals

A. Refuse and Liberate self from the Matriarchal rulebook of entanglements and dating[ii]
B. Boycott marriage and co-habitation, [iii] and in its place value my own life on my terms
C. Rejection of role as sole provider,[iv] protector[v] or pack mule in relationships
D. Recognize financial reality[vi] of relationships today, and in the future [vii viii]
E. Avoid costs of raising children; veto God's commandment to "go forth and multiply"
F. Defy societal male shaming techniques and slogans[ix x xi]

Each MGTOW member ***cannot*** be casually labeled. This would result in an inaccurate and unfair characterization of discrete MGTOW member's ideas, experience, knowledge, passions and unique backgrounds. MGTOW is a phenomenon that does not discriminate by age, ethnicity, political affiliation or other irrelevant factors. There are millions across the world who value a life of individual acceptance and freedom. This inclusiveness with freedom is a core value of Men Going Their Own Way.

# MGTOW History

Bachelorhood is nothing new. Even Paul the Apostle observed that wives and family can be an encumbrance. The current wave of MGTOW activity may have been inspired by Japanese Herbivores[xii], or "grass eaters." These are men who avoid permanent marital and romantic relationships.[xiii] The earliest reference to the tenets of MGTOW as an organized lifestyle was from a western newspaper entry in 1835. Herbivore men, the term itself, was first coined by Maki Fukasawa in an article published on Oct. 13, 2006. MGTOW became a buzzword in 2008 and 2009.[7][8][9][10] Since then, MGTOW has spread throughout every major nation.

# MGTOW Education

Men have to seek out MGTOW education and community where they can find it. Without political movements or women's and gender studies to teach men some of these concepts, men may not be exposed to these ideas; they aren't taught in schools, nor are they generally even talked or thought about. It is rare to come across any of the concepts unless you are actively seeking them out. A good place to start is online, they thrive on the Internet where an instructive and supportive sphere has formed. It is a coalition of sharing that fuels connection and consciousness. Social media (Facebook, Reddit, YouTube, forums, etc.) allow the MGTOW population and interested parties to bond.

Around 2008, marital failures and relationship difficulties were being publicly shared on various social media sites, including YouTube. Anonymous men with pseudonyms like Stardusk, Spetsnaz, Sandman and Barbarossa were a few of the forward-thinking innovators of the MGTOW YouTube phenomenon. Their videos shifted the paradigm of understood female nature and the videos attracted intense interest. Their social shifting ideas quickly spread to others. Now YouTube has hundreds of videos offering a daily dose of the Red Pill. This enlightened view of independence is mainly sustained by an individual brotherhood of men.

Websites devoted to this individual lifestyle are www.MGTOW.com,

Shedding the Ego (http://sheddingoftheego.com) and Happy Bachelors'
Forum (http://happybachelorsforum.com).

# Common Myths

1) **Men's Rights:** Some people believe that MGTOW is an ideology
   that splintered off from Men's Rights Advocacy (MRA). Previously,
   MGTOW may have been introduced through MRA connections.
   However, today most individuals discover the message through
   MGTOW social media channels and networks. Millions have
   found the MGTOW lifestyle, and some are *not* active political
   advocates for men's rights issues and instead focus on flourishing
   within the existing society.

2) **Sexless:** Some people claim MGTOW bans sex with women or it
   is a 'strike' that punishes women. A small group of MGTOW may
   be asexual, but most continue sexual relationships with women
   and have no interest in penalizing women.

3) **Anti-Social:** Others believe these men are hermits and want to
   move away from civilization. MGTOW are everywhere and live
   ordinary lives.

4) **Hate:** MGTOW is mistakenly considered as a "rage against
   women" and "misogynistic." But these men are actually
   discovering freedom, fulfillment of dreams, sex and love as they
   dodge the proverbial bullets of a culture that attempts to reinforce
   traditional dating and marriage contrivances. Although MGTOW
   members love women, this is a phenomenon about empowering
   and providing young men a safe place. Some MGTOW have
   suffered financial, physical and emotional pain in relationships,
   marriages and divorces, only to find MGTOW for emotional
   support. They are given a safe place to vent and then re-evaluate
   their life values.

5) **Wind Society Backwards:** Some think MGTOW is an attempt
   to take society backwards, creating a society of marital ownership
   and oppression of women. Instead, MGTOW is moving the male
   society forward and cultivating quality relationships between the

sexes. It creates an alternative future for men of all types and ages, and is a liberating force for young men, revealing a livable path before young men have suffered the blows of traditional masculine roles and marital relationship abuse.

6) **Gay, Cry Baby or Sissy:** The majority of the MGTOW population is straight but is inclusive to trans and gay people. They date and enjoy women and sex partners, but avoid any living arrangement that might douse their life ambitions and liberty. These individuals are not crying over previous injury, but are gaining power over their destiny. Each MGTOW individual creates his own path.

The following chapters are dedicated to millennials and any liberated man who has taken or might take the Red Pill. No matter how long the reader has shifted their societal lens, the author intends that some of these chapters will connect with them and be helpful in discovering joy, wealth and individual power.

⟫⟩◆⟨⟪

# CHAPTER 2

# Patriarchy Has No Gender

## How Patriarchy F*cked Men Up

**W**elcome MGTOW, bachelors, Herbivore men and curious others. Before journeying into our own millionairehood, we'll examine a shared brotherhood: patriarchy. We'll delve into masculinity, MGTOW character tools and speed through Jayden's college romance and then start counting our cash.

For as long as humanity has existed, we men have been under pressure to measure up to impossible standards of masculinity. We're raised to be strong, powerful and athletic. We're expected to be wealthy and emotionless. When we don't (or won't) live up to these fabricated standards, we run the risk of damaging our sense of self-worth. Even worse, the pressure to live up to an idealized version of manhood can invoke great stress and bring about intense feelings of shame, anxiety, depression and in the most extreme cases, can invoke suicidal tendencies.

This notion of "patriarchy" assumes that we men must be at the top of the power chain, providing and caring for women and children throughout our lives. Although various movements have sought to address how this framework oppresses women, the effects on us men are rarely, if ever, explored. Until our struggles are brought to light, little or nothing can be done to correct this imbalance and address what is, and always has been, a relentless burden.

To bring attention to this problem, it is necessary to first understand who is responsible for corralling men into the confines of hegemonic masculinity. For the most part, this gender "policing" is perpetrated by everyone, whether they are aware of it or not. Indeed, most of the time it is propagated by those we love most, including the women many of us spend our lives chasing. Not all women burden men with such expectations. But many girlfriends, wives and romantic partners wield this power over us like a battle sword. Without even realizing it.

## Women Perpetuating Patriarchy

Are women waging a secret a war on men? Ironically, it is the so-called 'weaker sex' whom nowadays are assuming the dominant role in intimate and other relationships. Women have taken it upon themselves to correct and discipline men the way they would scold and chide small boys. They say things like, "He's a little boy who needs to grow up and act like a man." Their weapon of choice is the sharpness of their tongues. Many are experts at inflicting emotional pain through words alone. Women employ tactics such as shaming and nagging which can stoke male insecurity and force even the most self-assured and independent men into submission—or worse. A 2014 study found, for example, that such verbal abuse was often a catalyst for husband suicides! [xiv]

Of course, some women don't necessarily realize the emasculating impact verbal violence can have on a spouse or significant other. As with patriarchy and other similar constructs, they are blindly led to believe that certain ways of thinking and acting are appropriate and reasonable. Even if they are not. And since they haven't, for various reasons, been themselves subjected to such abuse, they have little or no understanding of the damage such reckless behavior can cause. This doesn't mean all women should be let off the hook. There's no doubt a great many women are aware of the consequences of their actions and wield the power of verbal abuse as a tool to further their aims. So no matter if a person engaged in verbal abuse is aware of all the studies on the long term harm it cause, or if they are not aware of this; the use of such behavior is the problem of the abuser. The burden should be upon them to change.

Another paradox about patriarchy is that it has spawned broad social movements, which embrace the notion that women are more precious than men. The supposed theory behind such campaigns is to level the playing field between men and women; in reality the campaigns are often hijacked by extremists and the misinformed. The drive for equality of the sexes becomes a crusade to enforce a female advantage. So-called feminist movements have devolved into man-hating struggles for gender supremacy. While women try to make their purpose sound noble, their words often betray them. Just listen to their battle cries in popular media:

> *"R.E.S.P.E.C.T. ... I am woman ... Hear me roar ... Ladies first ... This is a woman's world ... Nobody can hold us down ... She dominates all access ... You don't own me ... We run this mutha ... If you like it, put a ring on it ... Who runs the world? GIRLS!.."*

Unfortunately, biological imperatives make the situation more complicated and difficult. Men easily comply with women's unreasonable and excessive demands because they're motivated by powerful and instinctual urges like sex. Society sees this as an acceptable form of coercion. We men will kowtow into submission, sacrificing our long-term health and financial wellbeing in the false belief that physical intimacy is our reward for being a "good" boy. In many respects we have become "vagina beggars," following lemming-like a dangerous course that ultimately proves fatal.

While women who support such behavior may not necessarily be to blame for the creation of such a framework, it seems clear that many females are more than happy to tag along without the foresight of thinking things through to conclusion. Certainly, the notion of patriarchy is long established, but surely they must take some of the blame for allowing it to propagate and influence the power structures in our homes and lives today.

A growing number of us guys are no longer okay with this arrangement. We've made a firm decision not to submit to the impossible standards that are designed solely to use men as a tool which often makes a male struggling in this role trying to be "good" feel like less of a man as time wears on. Millions have "taken the Red Pill"--Men Going Their Own Way (MGTOW), bachelors, Herbivore men and others--have decided to abandon these rules and notions of misconstrued tradition. Simply put, we no longer recognize the battle of the sexes nor the struggle for gender supremacy. We refuse to accept relationship structures that leave men and women at odds with one another. As of now, men can choose to be free from women's suffocating confines and are no longer held back by archaic principles and unrealistic expectations.

## The Beginning of Humans

Where did masculinity begin? Scientists across many disciplines estimate human beings first appeared in Africa about 200,000 years. Using evidence derived from the studies of archeology, geography and primatology, experts hypothesize certain social dynamics about our tribal ancestors. In virtually all known cases, the role of the male was that of provider and protector, whose strength and daring was crucial to the survival of his tribe.

Early humans could not survive without hard-earned life-sustaining essentials. This naturally led to the evolution of a societal hierarchy and members of the tribe took on tasks determined by a variety of characteristics such as proficiency, social role and other demands of time and ability. The family needed food, so everyone foraged. However, it was only men who possessed the physical and mental (memory/spacial) capabilities that allowed them to become expert hunters. Only the most revered, physically gifted and respected were capable of bringing home a fresh kill. Those who could not were considered inadequate and were consigned secondary, and generally less esteemed, roles. The successful hunters were the first alpha males of our species, comparable to today's breadwinners--those who "bring home the bacon."

There's little doubt that the evolution of the alpha male was inevitable and necessary at that time, as he was responsible for blazing a trail of survival through dangerous and unknown terrain. By virtue of their importance to the tribe, the biggest and strongest men were able to reproduce at the greatest rates over many generations. Everybody knew who they were. They could be picked out at a distance simply by observing their tone and stature. Over time, their offspring also became hunters as a rite of passage;

not surprisingly, they tended to be bigger and more powerfully built than the offspring of the less well endowed.

First as a matter of survival, and later as a matter of cultural conditioning, males who were smaller, thinner and weaker were shamed for being less than "real men." Males were there to protect and provide for their families and clan members of that gender who became frequently ill or who suffered from injury or disability were viewed by males and females alike as belonging to the lower echelons of society. Naturally, this encouraged even the most powerful and respected of the alpha males to suppress any hint or evidence of illness, injury or other limitations.

A man's worst fear was to be seen as something other than ideal and strong; any suggestion that he might be like a woman, whether because of passivity or effeminacy, was humiliating and a devastating insult. Any weakness could lead to conflict and possible death. Men lived in a state of perpetual fear of being seen to be weak or unfit. Over time, these and other perspectives solidified into the framework of a patriarchal hierarchy, where all men were measured against the archetype of the alpha male. Those at the top were revered and rewarded; those on the bottom were ignored or mistreated. Unfit, short, odd or disabled males were shamed because they couldn't perform what were seen as the most useful roles. They bowed down to the alpha and followed him as their leader.

Ordinary men of the tribe learned their role in the rank and file. This didn't necessarily mean blindly accepting their fate, however. The pressure to live up to tribal expectations or succumb to those who had proven themselves created endless anxiety deep inside. Ordinary men were constantly on guard for their standing in the clan and, ironically, it wasn't just those at the bottom who suffered. Alpha males were persistently under threat and alert to new challenges from younger, fitter males. They could never be sure who might confront them or when it might happen; the possibility of violent conflict was ever-present, evoking a completely and far more persistent kind of anxiety.

Man learned never to admit to weaknesses or faults, nor could he discuss such matters. The enormous pressure inevitably led to dark moods and depression. Some men began to engage in reckless, often self-destructive pursuits. And some committed suicide. It was a dangerous cycle that still continues today.

# The Mirror to Men

Just as men's roles became clearly institutionalized according to their standing in the tribe, a woman's need for food and security and her role in the reproductive process seemed to solidify into expected roles. As these roles became ingrained in society the whole process reinforced this behavior; evolving into patriarchy. Society in general sought out the strongest and most physically developed men. Women lived in constant fear of rape and violence. Accordingly, they would gather around the alphas like the flora and fauna that envelops a desert oasis. Alphas could have multiple women. Some women wantonly threw themselves at these "real men" in order to survive. Needless to say, individuals who were the object of such desires could not help but respond and act. Alpha male egos were stroked and so were their biological urges. The lesser males were left with only the scraps. The non-alphas lived with an endless terror of being last in line for food, warmth and women.

But most males also competed for the attention of females. Although feebler members could never hope to win the attention of the most desirable females, those more closely matching alpha traits felt the pressure to validate their masculinity at the expense of peers. The urge to reproduce and ensure one's genes would live on forever was a powerful driving force; women who provided males with children were coveted. And while the number of sexual couplings served to gauge a man's rank and capabilities, more often than not, it was the woman who decided which partner was or wasn't good enough to use for reproduction.

Therefore we can see that these social dynamics encouraged even those males who were less than alpha to go to great lengths to attract females and please them any way they could. Such an interest could help them overcome other masculine shortcomings and validate their maleness. For example, if she noticed, winked or smiled at him, it was as if his status as a real man had been suddenly improved. If he had women chasing him, others might perceive him to be the genuine article, even if, by one measure or another, he wasn't.

# Centuries of History

Through the centuries, alpha males became the leaders, kings, pharaohs and emperors, gaining and expanding their power over others. Whether by force or by the sheer misfortune of their status, males in the lower tiers became indentured, in some cases literally, to support and revere those at the top. Men built monuments, palaces, religious shrines and labored to create the wonders of the world. From the great Pyramids of Egypt, to the Hanging Gardens of Babylon, to the Statue of Zeus in Greece - the lowliest men have toiled and slaved. But they weren't just builders; many were drafted or co-opted to fight ugly wars and respond to violent threats from rival nations and leaders. Much blood has been shed, many lives have been broken, and entire civilizations have been toppled in the name of real men.

Males not eligible for the role of warrior or soldier or other such masculine pursuits sought other ways to serve in order to compensate for their shortcomings. Many became artists, inventors and merchants, or they cultivated skills that could, in one way or another, provide a benefit to society. Apart from their omnipotent role of 'mother' which females have exclusive enjoyment on over the ages, food preparation and home upkeep were women's main tasks. Motherhood was enjoyed and some twisted this role to their own advantage. Whether it was because men have been better conditioned or have innate capabilities not shared by women, masculinity has been an institutionalized value running through the construction of great cities and countries. Masculinity has developed the dependable accessories of everyday living and the technological brilliance that has launched astronauts into space and rocket ships to Mars.

# The Men of Today

Civilization has developed into giant metropolises each interconnected with the other via supplies, technology, culture and fast transportation. Yet the artifacts and framework of our patriarchal past remain with us like the ruins of dead cities made of clay. Men are trapped in a never-ending charade of trying to prove our worth to women and to other men according to pre-historical values. Meanwhile, most remain willing participants in what has become a modern version of the battle between the sexes. Women exploit their own sexuality and tempt and test us with the one-sided demands of a relationship designed totally in their interests. With endless complaints and arguments, they like to see how we hold up under pressure; if we fail they move on and seek out a male they can control. They probe to see if they can take advantage of the many constraints that have been heaped upon men from the earliest days of mankind.

## The Cost of Being Her King

Needless to say, the more attractive the female, the more power she wields over us men. Urged on by the powerful instincts that are essential to the survival of our species, we have elevated beautiful females to the status of goddesses, and we worship them as if sexual companionship is our sole purpose. A man will do anything for a woman if she makes him feel masculine, whether that means working long hours at dirty jobs to keep her in the luxury she demands or fighting with others to prove our loyalty. Men are often expected to pay for her attention. If he suspects he's lacking in some way, he will feel compelled to make up the difference so as not to find himself in the demeaning position of being without a relationship that validates his status.

Since most women are by nature weak and vulnerable in the face of physical violence, many naturally crave the security only a 'real man' can offer. Some women willfully push their men into dangerous or difficult situations so they can "prove" they are the tough and strong protectors of old. The classic example of this "protector" stereotype is the "damsel in distress" storyline. Whenever a woman is in a situation she appears unable to get out of, or even when she feigns fear or anguish, it can trigger a "superman" reaction in men. When women cry help or rape, our guts twist, our empathy spikes and we automatically race to the rescue. These are techniques women have used since the dawn of time to invoke compassion for their physical needs and their emotional and political causes. Like the alpha males of the ancient tribes, men can be the hero who rescues her from life's dark forces. Sadly, his only reward may be a smile or a kiss on the cheek.

Most women's nature and central role in raising children has inevitably reinforced a belief among both sexes that women must be protected and provided for, and that it is men or the government who must assume this role. But it's men who must continually prove our intentions and our ability to perform the functions we were supposedly designed for. Whether paying for flowers, romantic dates, expensive diamond rings or lavish weddings; we must convince females that we can live up to "a good man's" responsibilities--and a lot more. As with other constructs of the patriarchal hierarchy, the beneficiaries of such treatment have been conditioned to expect as much because our culture says this is how real men behave. From the time small girls watch their first Disney princess movie, women are taught that they should be treated like royalty.

## Men Gave the Power Away

The distorted realities of our patriarchal past and the relentless pressures of hegemonic masculinity have, to put it bluntly, fucked us guys up. While some women may claim they are against such a system--with a few actually meaning it--their failure to step back and take time to understand the role that their words, actions and mindset have played in creating such a situation only serves to perpetuate our misery. Many of us have become the lapdogs of feminine abuse, unable to free ourselves of the weighty chains that continually hold us down.

In recent decades, instead of equality, the majority of women have sought advantage. Many have recklessly wielded their power and seductive influence to bring us males down and manipulate us into submission and obedience. Women humiliate us publicly, telling anyone who will listen how stupid, childlike, incapable and bumbling we are. It is sadly not uncommon for a man to be driven to take his own life simply to escape the continual verbal barrage of a nagging wife. [xv] If we survive the verbal assaults in marriage, when wives' divorce us, it is also one of the top reasons we commit suicide.[xvi] Rampant misandry is everywhere--in the media, in schools, the workplace and our homes. The media is vindictive, endlessly using men as the butt of jokes. Women have defined man's status and where he stands in the greater order of things. They prey on our vulnerabilities and utilize their feminine wiles to perpetuate grotesque stereotypes and a destructive dependence on lopsided intimacy.

## Liberation: Discovering Happiness

But as songwriter Bob Dylan once wrote, *the times they are a-changin'*. Years of denigration and abuse have taken their toll and many of us males have begun to ask questions. Do we deserve to be treated so poorly? Are our needs subservient to theirs? Are we merely indentured servants, waiting hand and foot, completely at women's beck and call? Are we supposed to sit back and become totally marginalized, like the males in the matriarchal African villages whose all-female leaders recently relegated all men to the lowest rungs of the social ladder?[xvii] Will we become nothing more than "manginas," capriciously and carelessly manipulated at the whim of our female captors?

For a growing number of men, the answer is a resounding "**no!**" After centuries of enslavement, we are angry as hell! We will not take it anymore! A tsunami of male sovereignty is sweeping across the planet and we are grabbing the proverbial sword of opportunity to enlighten ourselves. We are demanding liberation from the prison of a primitive and archaic social order. Men are speaking out and seeking to empower other men to break free from the bonds of patriarchal expectations. We are refusing to subjugate ourselves to relationships where women manipulate myopic monogamy to the detriment of our freedom and souls. We are seeking to express and enjoy our deepest interests, rather than toiling endlessly in the pursuit of a life that leads to relationship unhappiness and inequality.

This is a new and exciting world for us men. A world where we can finally do what we want and work at the things we love. Whether we enjoy tinkering with automobiles, flying kites, dancing in a ballet, kicking back and playing sports or grooming ourselves so that we may, by choice rather than compulsion, become leaders, inventors and creators; it doesn't matter. We are realizing our right to self-define who we are and choose our higher purpose. Men are amazing, and we have the qualities and drive to change the world--only now, it is our decision to make. No longer condemned to live a life dictated by women and ancient roles, we can shed the debilitating confines of social expectation and truly enjoy the fruits of our labors.

## Patriarchy is a Myth

The idea that the corridors of power are all-male is an ancient, outdated relic. Today our political and business world is diverse where women rule 23 of the world's countries.[xviii] Positions are open to all and in the United States 296 women fill positions in the federal government and 3,859 fill state positions.[xix] Ethnic and gender diversity peppers the American political halls of power. In 2016, two women are running for the most powerful office in the world: the President of the United States. Women are more likely to get a college degree and fill over 58% of all American jobs.[xx] Approximately ten million American women are CEOs, owning their own companies and corporations.[xxi] The idea that we live in a society where men systemically and institutionally dominate women is painting the world with a discriminating broad brush. It is a sexist stereotype. It has not kept up with the changing times.

Any woman who walks in a short dark-skinned man's shoes would experience more sexism, racism, discrimination and oppression in one month than she would in a lifetime in her own skin. Our societies may never have exact parity or equality between classes, races and genders. Any of us can use a critical gendered lens to see what they want. A better use of our time would be to reach out and help a friend or neighbor, no matter their race or gender. There will come a day when each of us will need a friend.

## Finding Manhood

Our higher education system, namely in the Women's and Gender Studies departments, is concentrating on including critical thinking about masculinity.

# CHAPTER 3

# Masculinity

Reducing the notion of masculinity to a handful of characteristics is a fool's errand. Each of us has masculine and feminine attributes, mixed together into an individual cocktail that we call "human."

We haven't begun our guide on budgeting, saving, investing and amassing assets and power yet. There's still something we must ask first. As men, we are sometimes unsure about how to interact with the world around us, but why is that? Young or old, why are we confused or conflicted about what it means to "be a man?" Without getting lost in a myriad of details, the goal of this chapter is to outline some of the characteristics that define this notion. Masculinity is not the stereotype of a porn star, athlete or superhero: it can take many forms that vary between us. As Norman Mailer once said, *"Masculinity is not something given to you, but something you gain. And you gain it by winning small battles with honor."*

## Violent Masculinity

Despite what some say, masculinity does not mean violent. And yet, a militant segment of society repeatedly claims that our nature is responsible for such acts, especially against women. In recent years, some extremists have launched matriarchal attacks on what they mistakenly characterize as masculinity; in colleges nationwide, textbooks and courses attempt to validate this view of men as innately violent. Academics are collating skewed data, seeking to prove the demeaning assertion that masculinity is the source of violence and threats against women.

Many "gender studies" books and curricula use clever misdirection to "prove" their assertions. They rely on definitions like those put forth by authors Victoria Pruin DeFrancisco and Catherine H. (Helen) Palczewski in which they define "violence" as intimidation, emotional, verbal and physical abuse, sexual assault and murder, and then carry out surveys of only women that show 70% have suffered violence at our hands. But the authors do not survey us and usually fail to mention the flaws in the survey, suggesting that it is only women who have experienced such a fate. In fact, it is likely that a survey of men would find 90% of them reporting that they had been treated violently, given that intimidation and verbal abuse fall under that heading.

Domestic violence is one of society's gravest ills but it is not a masculine problem. In fact, it is not uncommon to see women lashing out in anger, slashing tires, destroying personal effects or throwing us out of our homes. Evidence suggests that couples, whether they are of the opposite or same sex, argue and strike one another for various reasons and with alarming regularity. In many cases, the source of the problem is money or jealousy; other times, one or both may be suffering from mental illness or substance abuse. Couples have always argued, but perhaps those who lose control are unfit for any sort of relationship. In those cases, verbal assaults can quickly escalate until there is slapping, hitting, shoving--or worse.

## How Militants Inspire Distrust in Men

Over the course of recent decades, equality movements have spurred major advancements for women. In America for example, more women than men currently attend college or are employed in the workforce. Arguably, women's and gender studies have facilitated this evolution. But is it not also true that equal rights have led to greater injustice for men? As with many such ideologies, a radicalized minority has co-opted those movements; they have broadcast a biased message of how men interact with and "victimize" women. These propagandists repeat as fact the myth of women as victims of male domination, going so far as to deny a history where women have often played a dominant role.

Even some women are aware of the blatant manipulations and distortions that have occurred. As doctor and feminist Janice Fiamengo once said on a popular Canadian TV show, *Charles Adler, "The field of women's studies is a man-blaming, if not a man-hating ideology. It is about indoctrination into an ideology and is not scholarly or factual. Women's and gender studies uses statistics that are dubious. It advances a world view of women's moral superiority as innocent victims of male violence. It advances the idea that men are overwhelmingly brutal, aggressive and dominant."*

In reality, such teachings can inspire distrust, disgust and hatred toward men--all men. Women's and gender studies could do much better for students and the world at large by being more inclusive and less focused on dishing out repugnance for a hetro-normative white male. A call to the higher angels of moderate voices is needed and a comprehensive study of all genders would benefit all of society. Unfortunately, the narrow gender lens they rely on is simply too sexist and, quite often, blatantly racist. Interestingly, in juxtaposition to these shaky teachings, research suggests that female couples are the most violent,[xxii] with the highest recorded rate of domestic violence among them. And yet, this issue is mostly ignored by academia. Other studies reveal that there has been a virtual epidemic of women teachers and guards sexually assaulting and committing statutory rape upon teen boys in middle schools and juvenile detention centers,[xxiii] but this is not a topic that seems to warrant attention.

Over time, the field of gender studies will need to change. After years of lopsided conversation, it is likely that we will see more diverse, inclusive and fairer discussions of gender and race going forward. But if we are going to genuinely reduce all categories of rape and domestic violence, then college administrations and boards of regents will need to grapple with the existing bias.

## Social Masculinity

Every one of us has likely heard such things as, "Step up! Be a man! Man up!" or simply, "Suck it up!" But what do these words mean? In reality, we are often undermined by seemingly endless definitions of masculinity. Where is the how-to guide that shows us the way to behave? Other than the barrage of impromptu rules and scoldings we've endured throughout our lives from well-intentioned mothers, grandmothers, girlfriends and wives, how exactly are we supposed to learn our role in society? Most of us work hard to make money and pay the bills; many of us strive to have comfortable homes and nice cars. But why do we do it? Are these things the outward manifestations of masculinity? Are they the outward manifestations of items we really enjoy? Do we interact with the world in this way because our fathers and grandfathers did? Or is it simply because this is what society has forced upon us?

As men, we are supposed to grow up as quickly as possible. We're expected to find a woman, marry her and make her happy. For millions of us, these social dogmas have proved to be disastrous. Does our partner pull her weight, or is it left for us to do the lion's share of the work, earn the money, fix the house--provide, provide, provide? What are we getting in return, besides an occasional round of hurried sex? Today, with almost half of marriages ending in divorce, men are waking up to the social injustice society calls the 'matrimonial institution.' We are finally saying "No!" to oppression. Around the world, we are beginning to follow our own paths and reaching for dreams by our own artistic design.

## Benefits of Masculinity

But even with this evolution, it is hard to ignore the mindset that brought us to this place, or why many people apparently believe that the world does not benefit from masculinity in its other forms. It is such an inherently natural phenomenon that we--men--hardly ever think about it. Women, however, often claim to find masculinity foreign and frightening. Ironically, some women have aggression and traits of masculinity running through their veins, and they are considered assets to society, while many trans-men are simply amazing! Whoever finds masculinity coursing through their spirit or playing a dominant role within them should consider themselves lucky and gifted. Take advantage of it!

As men, we are blessed with certain abilities. None of us should quash our nature, because suppression is never good. None of us must subvert true energy: we can and should choose to develop, mold and embrace any of the masculine characteristics that are swirling within us. Unfortunately, many females have taken it upon themselves to establish alternative benchmarks that we must measure up to. Mother's train and discipline us early in life; later, our girlfriends and wives continue to try to tame the supposed beast within us. In college, one-sided policies dictate our behavior: we must be politically correct and understand that "no means no" seminars are aimed at men. Only, woman can be the abusers too, but we are not taught that fact when young men are being molded as to how to behave properly.

But now, men are defining their own masculinity; those who are not born male cannot define it for us. This is our wheelhouse. We are the gods of this sphere and they have no power here. We do not have a uterus and, consequently, many of us have done what's right and stayed away from debates about abortion and what females should do with their bodies, minds and souls. All we have ever asked for in return is fairness and equality. Feminist Camille Paglia once said, *"Manhood coerced into sensitivity is no manhood at all."* Nature tells us that the powerful miracle of manhood is meant for far more than it has been allowed before now.

## Question Everything

Men and boys love to explore and question the universe, and they learn from a very early age that there are always two sides to a story. Being empathetic and looking at things from different perspectives can reveal surprising details about the way of the world. An inquisitive mind helps us to navigate through a world saturated with crosscurrents of conflicting media, data and facts. The quest for knowledge is the foundation of science. We yearn to understand life and its various elements in order to formulate a more balanced and accurate picture of events. Such an approach enables us develop the prowess required to make better decisions. As Bryant H. McGill once remarked, *"One of the most important things one can do in life is to brutally question every single thing you are taught."*

# Emotional Masculinity

Women process emotional harms differently than men. Some will remember every micro-aggressive word said to them in their lives. If, for example, Claire asks her friend, Martha, "Did you gain weight?" the latter might store the harmless inquiry as a painful injury. From then on, Martha might view everything her friend says as a subversive or hurtful jab. Ten years later, Martha might blow up in a fit of rage and spew it all back at Claire as though she were a volcano of pent-up hate. Men, however, are more robust. For us, the art of digs and jabs is an enjoyable pastime; more often than not, such remarks are sport and are nothing more than a test of another's battle-wear, nothing of insult meant in the short or long term.

Perhaps because of this, we men are often viewed as being non-emotional. Masculinity is a useful component of our lives and essential to cultivating our inner selves, but emotions are also an important and vital factor to our psyche, which we would do well to explore. In reality, the square-jawed, hard-eyed, and inarticulate Hollywood stereotype is just another box that the world tries to squeeze us into. We feel things deeply, but we process those feelings differently than women. Real men don't have to be rocks all the time; in fact, it's smart not to be. Indeed, World Cup skier Marcel Hirscher summed it up beautifully: *"It's incredible how many emotions you feel when crossing the finish line and seeing that you are No. 1."*

As intelligent men, we need to be open-minded about culture and trends. It's perfectly acceptable for us to enjoy art, beauty, music and dance. By following our feelings, we can savor an amazing life filled with rich experiences, regardless of whether we laugh or cry. Our emotions prove we are human; without them, we're nothing but robots, unable to accomplish anything meaningful.

# Breakthrough all Fears

Some people run from fear; others seek safe havens, hunkering down to ride out the storm. Regardless, everyone feels such an emotion at some point in their lives. As boys, many of us undoubtedly experienced it at every age, but we are rarely taught how to deal with it appropriately.

Being afraid is a fundamental aspect of survival and is closely tied to our instinctive fight-or-flight response. It is a warning system that reminds us to proceed with caution; to examine alternatives as we move forward. As Franklin D. Roosevelt said, *"The only thing we have to fear is fear itself."* Hiding is often not the answer; running away rarely leads to growth.

But fear can be conquered. Toddlers and infants might recoil from loud noises, unfamiliar objects and strangers, while older boys can be frightened of the dark, sounds in the night, masks, monsters and ghosts. But when they become men like us, those fears have generally been overcome. Growing up helps each of us understand that the dark mysteries of our youth are no mystery at all. Once they become familiar to us, our fears tend to fade and subside. Sure, as grown men we can still be afraid, but our maturity helps us to better handle that fear. Instead of hiding under the covers, we try to understand. We drag the fear out into the light and analyze it. By so doing, we conquer it.

Psychology books are full of explanations and treatments for fears and phobias of every kind. Some remedies are based on finding out what is behind them. In other cases, it is best to confront them. For those of us who have a fear of heights, forcing ourselves to the top of a skyscraper can cause the fear to melt away. Through persistence and courage, we can face such obstacles. If we are scared, we must move forward anyway, one step at a time. Taking such risks, whether physical, mental or emotional, can help us develop valuable abilities. That doesn't mean being reckless, of course. It is important to think about the consequences if we should fail, and to always keep other options in mind.

Through our interaction with others we learn to adapt and evolve. Rolling with life's punches and reacting to changes in our environment is the essence of moving forward. We have either been socially groomed or designed by nature to fight to survive, so why don't we utilize this natural talent? Emotional growth requires facing our problems and fears head on and learning from them. So, we need to break through the barriers of our own angst to grab our fears by the throat and squeeze hard. In the end, we might be surprised: maybe they weren't that scary after all.

# Men Moving Forward

We've discussed the levers that can be pulled to manage ourselves as masculine. We've looked at how some people demonize masculinity while men have delivered great social benefits using this same masculinity. We've learned to question everything, to adapt and empower our physical machine. By discussing the buttons that can be pushed—emotional maturity and breakthrough of fears--we embrace our masculinity. All of us are able to use our uniquely individual power and change our world. In the next chapter we will learn about our innate powers.

# Chapter 4

# Individual Power

We live in an exciting era of opportunity and innovation. We have the power and ability to shape the future of our planet. Once free from the pursuits of youth, we can find and define our place in the universe and begin to build wealth. Our power to navigate is vital. As men, we have myriad capabilities that we can develop and deploy. The single life of freedom leads us to doors that allow us to experiment and live. Which should we open? What direction should we take? What journey besieges us? Francis Bacon once said, *"Knowledge is power."* Before we can move forward to our financial plan of action, we must understand the powers we have and learn about the time-worn MGTOW character tools that empower us to visualize and create things that might have once seemed unimaginable.

## Mental Health is Physical Health

From an evolutionary point of view, men are gifted machines, bestowed with attributes and abilities that can help us move mountains. We possess the physical structure and dexterity to accomplish tasks that, at first glance, seem undoable. Not all of us have superior musculature, of course. But regardless of whether we are naturally blessed with muscles or not, we owe it to ourselves to nurture and enhance our physical being, and to maintain it as meticulously as we would a finely-tuned engine. We should encourage boys with spirited behavior, not reprimand them for being hyperactive. Physical exertion is how young men ascertain their limits. We should care for our human apparatus just as we would a rare Ferrari, cleaning and tuning ourselves up at least three times a week. As President John F. Kennedy noted, *"Physical fitness is not only one of the most important keys to a healthy body, it is the basis of dynamic and creative intellectual activity."*

> **MGTOW character tool number one:** Maintain a healthy body. It's important to walk, stretch, body build and workout in order to realize our future potential. Being clean and healthy allows us to reap the benefits of our manhood, enhancing our power and self-esteem in the process.

Whether through social programming or DNA, many of us are born engineers, naturally designed to create and construct things. The way our brains and physical nature have developed over time has enabled us to actively shape the world we live in. We are hard-wired to evaluate situations, recognize problems and overcome them. We are results-oriented beings. If we want to get from A to B, we build a road; if we want shelter from the elements, we build a house. We construct bridges to span obstacles and invent machines to do our work more efficiently. But it doesn't stop there. If we look around our homes, we can see a range of tools and appliances designed by men to make life easier. We have carefully engineered even the *most basic* necessities of life, which both men and women alike would be lost without. If you are gifted with such abilities, embrace them.

We don't just create for the sake of creating. We are also predisposed to examine and improve our environment, not just for ourselves, but for others, most of whom we don't even know. We give to our communities and strive, unselfishly, to make life on earth richer and more comfortable for all. We do it because we can, and we do it for the benefit of the greater good.

# Don't Grow Up

Have you ever seen a child encounter something for the first time? Have you noticed how their eyes widen in joyful awe at the newfound discovery? Small children are able to face the unknown with a sense of wonder and fearlessness. Success sometimes requires us to remain childlike, to retain that sense of wonder. Sometimes it means we have to believe in magic, or in things that seem far out of reach. Take the Wright brothers, for example. Back in the early 1900s, the whole idea of manned, mechanized flight must have seemed like utter madness to the masses. But the brothers never lost their belief in the dream --despite the ridicule, despite the derision of their peers, they persevered.

Men and boys are often told to "grow up" or "act your age." Society wants us to set aside our hobbies, toys and childish behaviors, even though this can cause us to lose our sense of wonder and force us to see the world through jaded eyes. What exactly do the words mean? Get a job and pay the bills? Give up our hobbies and repair the roof? Drop imagination and live a stiff and pre-planned life? Sadly, many of us succumb to such expectations. Why? Are we expected to labor our precious days away and dull the pain in ways that only hurt us? The answer is "no." In the words of Pablo Picasso, " ...every child is an artist. The problem is how to remain an artist once we grow up."

> **MGTOW character tool number two:** Embrace the magic of our childhood--again. We can harness immense power by doing so. As John Cleese wisely noted, " ...*the most creative people have this childlike facility to play.*"

A man's hobby can be the doorway to his dreams. Visions and aspirations give us hope and allow us to express ourselves in a very personal way. Whatever our passion is--whether it's collecting postage stamps or baseball cards, building model railways, fly fishing, tinkering with automobiles or studying quantum theory--we must live it and breathe it whenever and however we can. Hold on to the inner child and don't ever allow anyone to tell us that it's wrong. That, my friend, is what it means to be all grown up!

# Men and Boys Have Dreams Too

Martin Luther King, Jr. "had a dream" and because of this, he was a powerful man. Finding and following our dreams is our key to success. Just like girls, we imagine what we would like to see, do and be when we grow up. But our dreams can be vastly different than theirs. Boys might dream of being a race car driver, astronaut, rock star or famous athlete. Girls, on the other hand, might dream of getting married, having children and living with a family in a nice home--or of being in charge, the family matriarch. Unfortunately, as our life unfolds before us, we are often drawn away into others' dreams. Sometimes, it seems like there is only one socially acceptable outcome: marriage. But that is not true.

> **MGTOW character tool number three:** Nurture your dreams and live them the best way you can. Walt Disney said, "*If you can dream it, you can do it.*" Remember, your dreams are an inner power.

More often than not, entanglements with a woman force us to make tradeoffs. We are asked to sacrifice *our* dreams for hers or those of a family, and to give them a lion's share of our time and energy. While it doesn't take long for us to realize when the spark is gone, we may allow ourselves to remain trapped in such situations because of societal obligations which only drain our time and resources. Her claims of moral authority and family demands can easily exhaust our abilities and cause us to lose sight of ourselves. Unable to live out our own dreams, many of us will acquiesce to carrying out theirs. We are expected to encourage them to follow their desires, to provide emotional support and to work ourselves to the bone whenever necessary. This invariably leads to deep frustration, eventually wearing us out.

# Mastery: Practice, Practice, Practice

Everyone makes mistakes on the journey towards achieving their goals and ambitions, but such errors can be opportunities if we choose learn from them. As Joyce Meyer once pondered, "*I wonder how many times people give up just before a breakthrough--when they are on the very brink of success."* Problems also represent opportunities in disguise. Setbacks and breakdowns are reasons to assess and redirect our efforts; they are not without purpose. Indeed, physical and emotional strength often come from a succession of failures. Whether it's getting a bad grade at school, our inability to knock a minute off that three-mile run or letting down a friend, failure is what teaches us about others and ourselves.

> **MGTOW character tool number four:** Master the thing that you love. To gain or maintain proficiency in it, practice and learn as much as you can. Have complete power over your art.

Most of us strive toward self-improvement. Mastering certain skills or acquiring specific knowledge can boost our confidence and reinforce our independence. But such things don't happen by magic. As Mahatma Gandhi said, *"An ounce of practice is worth more than tons of preaching."* Almost everything in life involves some measure of trial and error; it is only though persistence and determination, evaluating each less-than-perfect try, that we can anticipate success. Men love to compete, but winning and personal growth require considerable practice. While virtually anyone can achieve a certain level of proficiency and expertise in whatever field they choose, the old saying, "practice makes perfect," continues to hold true.

In the end, each of us must be our own man, where perfection is uniquely defined. Each time we attempt something; we must assess our weaknesses and imperfections, and then strive to overcome them. In addition, what is considered weak or imperfect must be defined differently according to our differing life goals! We need to leverage the knowledge and experience we gain, the lessons we learn, and the MGTOW character traits we develop by persisting until we achieve our goal. These are the hidden prizes, empowering us with new talents and knowledge that will remain with us for the rest of our lives. They change who we are--for the better.

# Strength and Courage

Physical prowess is not the only advantage that we have. We are also able to use our *strength of will* to overcome challenges in the natural environment, predators and other adversaries, although it's worth remembering that strength is not violence. In the words of Abraham Lincoln, *"Be sure you put your feet in the right place, then stand firm."*

> **MGTOW character tool number five:** Willpower is a formidable internal muscle. It reinforces character, furthers fortitude and provides us with foresight and vision.

Strength also means stamina. It's the quality that motivates us to put in the extra hours required to meet a deadline, or to travel great distances to seal a deal. Mental strength enables us to hold fast to our ideals and freedoms. It is not blind persistence, however; it also helps us know when to call, raise or fold--the difference between letting your stake ride or cashing out.

Our physical capabilities allow us to stand up to external forces, confront danger and survive, conquer foes and, in a very real sense, move mountains. But it's our willpower that keeps us going long after others have thrown in the towel. The best example, perhaps, could be seen in a speech by British Prime Minister Winston Churchill during the Second World War, when he succeeded in rallying his countrymen around him during his nation's darkest hour. Faced with the prospect of an imminent Nazi invasion, the odds stacked against them, Churchill uttered his famous words: " *...we shall fight on the seas and oceans ... we shall defend our island whatever the cost may be. We shall fight on the beaches ... we shall fight in the fields and streets ... we shall never surrender!"*

It worked. Churchill's fiery battle cry inspired the British to hold out long enough for the United States to come to their rescue, and together the two great nations went on to defeat Hitler and save the world from a fascist future. It is a moment in time that we should not forget. It should also serve as a constant reminder in our own lives: we are men, and we never give up. Whether we are soldiers fighting on the front lines, or we are average Joes, pushing hours of overtime just to survive, we have the power to control destiny--ours and others'.

**MGTOW character tool number six:** We are men. We never give up.

Even when we know there are great risks ahead, we regularly decide to stay the course. We have the will to think beyond the threats to ourselves in order to help others. True courage is the noble virtue of doing what is morally right, such as running into a burning building to save a pet dog. The passion to do what is right may drive our courage to accomplish our goals; it's good for our mind, body and soul. Courage is the will to persist and hold ground until we have achieved our goals, despite the risk of failure.

## Change is Fundamental

Our civilization is advancing at a faster pace than ever before, and in the process, many of us are rethinking how we relate to and live with others, especially those of the opposite sex. The natural emergence of millions of Herbivore men, single moms, MGTOWs and gender social justice warriors may well be an indication that the constructs of mating, socializing and living situations are evolving. Does this represent a shift in the dynamics between the sexes? Is this the tip of an iceberg of a transition to a new societal structure of families and social ties? Animal groups have evolved over millions of years and adapted how families cohabitate. Are we experiencing a more rapid progression regarding our ways of life-spaces? It seems that some parts of society are adopting new ideas of family and safe spaces for gender-specific groups.

In a changing world, men race to keep up with a relentless stream of life-altering events and technological innovations. Though we struggle to further personal, emotional and social maturity, we must remember that the best way to grow is still the easiest: through new friends. When we meet someone new it is like falling in love--again. Every friend opens our eyes and makes our heart beat faster. We should experience this love of friends, brothers, sisters and gods as often as possible. Each person who shares a part of themselves with us becomes an integral piece of our soul.

> **MGTOW character tool number seven:** Meet new people, and help yourself--and them--to grow. As Bill Gates once noted, *"We all need people to give us feedback. That's how we improve."*

The people we allow to become a part of our lives may influence us more than we know. They give us buoyancy and new energy. We often discover something good in them that can bring out a similar quality in us. Having close friends can help us round out our personality and deepen our experience. As we go through life, it's these 'people experiences' that define our uber-selves. No matter how dire our circumstances, meeting and making new friends, learning from them and learning to love them--being a "people person"--can provide us with the skills and intellectual tools necessary to expand our social horizons and enhance our emotional growth.

## Mastery of Engineering, Science and Technology

Plato once said, *"Necessity ... is the mother of invention."* From primitive origins, our forebears went on to harness fire and master their natural surroundings. Thankfully, they also learned invaluable skills from oppressive kings, pharaohs and emperors, who used men to build the incredible wonders of the world. Those ancient practices allowed us to harness our natural masculine strengths to conquer, engineer and become the builders of great societies. To some, engineering is only a technical skill, but as Queen Elizabeth II noted, *"At its heart, engineering is about using science to find creative, practical solutions. It is a noble profession."*

We and our ancestors have transformed accidental discoveries and the inspirations of madmen, fools and dreamers into realities and miracles that make our life what it is today. Varieties of flora and fauna became the bedrocks of modern pharmacology; witch doctors and faith healers became our doctors and spiritual guides. A wide range of medical advances have boosted our average life expectancy to more than 80 years of age.

Women were liberated from the bonds of pregnancy, birthing and nurturing unwanted children by a man-made discovery: the birth control pill.[xxiv] Many historians credit The Pill as the most important mechanism for transferring control over reproductive rights from men to women. Today, women are better able to join alongside men to co-create and engineer the advances that can help to ensure our future progress. Though men have long led humanity in the sciences and technology, improving life for everyone in the process, any one of us who is so inclined should be encouraged to take the reins.

Still, we are the ones who should take credit for where we are today. Our legacy is the infrastructure, knowledge and technology that have been left behind after the inventors and builders have passed on. As Tina Turner said, *"My legacy is that I stayed on course ... from the beginning to the end, because I believed in something inside of me."*

> **MGTOW character tool number eight:** Look both within and outside of you. See what your own legacy might be.

## Inventing our Future

Some of us are taking charge of our destinies. We have escaped others' expectations. We are free, smelling the sweet scent of liberated air. The pain of the past is still there, though newfound freedom heals the wounds. But what's next? Once liberated, we might feel confused or experience an inner void. There is no roadmap to travel such a road. There are no road signs saying, "Bachelors, this way!" Where do we go from here?

Bachelorhood is not a path. It is a lifestyle. It is not something that we can read about in a book. It is a mission that each of us joyfully invents. Remember those childhood dreams? Remember that vision deep inside of us that we stuffed away for someone else's benefit? Bryant H. McGill said, *"Creativity is the greatest expression of liberty."* We are creators, givers and builders. Freedom allows us the opportunity to bring about what we want. We are free to pen our own script, our special screenplay.

**MGTOW character tool number nine:** Do what you love and are passionate about. Find your real vocation and purpose. If you toil away at what nurtures you and makes you happy, you'll be rejuvenated, not worn out.

## How to Solve Your Problems

There's no doubt that many of the problems we face can be difficult to solve. They can be formidable barriers to achieving our aspirations or even conceiving new dreams. But we are natural problem solvers--we fix things. While life may sometimes overwhelm us with a seemingly endless stream of hurdles and roadblocks, we cannot let them hold us back. When we wrestle with issues that block us from reaching our goals, we must move beyond them and release the powerful forces within ourselves.

**MGTOW character tool number ten:** Each of us has an automatic control system, cybernetics, built into our brain's neurons. It is a powerful tool that can help us overcome challenges while we sleep!

Many people don't know about the workings of the brain or how to engage it in solving various problems. But we have neurological capabilities that are like our own personal supercomputers. Suppose, for example, we are considering any number of the following questions:

*Should I move to North Dakota and work in the oil fields?*
*Should I divorce my wife?*
*Is it time to move to Arizona?*
*Is bankruptcy the right thing?*
*Should I repair a broken relationship?*
*Should I take a new class at the college to learn to weld?*
*Should I invest in a new home?*

By placing such dilemmas at the forefront of our consciousness before going to bed, we can capitalize on our brain's natural problem-solving capabilities. As we sleep, our minds automatically process events and information from our time awake. Certain data get moved to long-term memory storage, cleaning and freeing up short-term space. During sleep, the brain shuffles data around, organizing and clarifying. As the night progresses, our minds address any issues or concerns raised, and gradually problems begin to unravel themselves. When we wake up in the morning, all of a sudden, the answers will be obvious. We will know the decisions to be made, allowing us to move forward.

## Creating Reality with Intention

Werner Erhard, the renowned academic from the 1970s human potential movement, once noted that, " ...*personal power is the ability to translate intention into reality.*" It seems that some of us amble through our day-to-day existence constantly disempowering ourselves, finding ways to impede and complicate our lives with challenges, never learning how to translate intentions into that which we desire.

The fact is, virtually everything in our modern, man-made lives began as just an idea. But such notions can't become palpable without being transformed by intention. It is our *intention ability* that enables us to define and create reality. It is also like a muscle in our brains: the more we use it, the stronger it gets. Instead of merely processing stimuli, we can use our focus to create something tangible. Albert Einstein, the Nobel prize-winning scientist, relied on such a technique when he developed his theories about the universe. So, too, did other men, including Archimedes, Nikola Tesla and Henry Ford. They harnessed great power from directing their conscious and daydreaming minds in a singular direction.

**MGTOW character tool number eleven:** Our minds are engines of creation, allowing us to define who we are and what we want to be in the future. All that is required is time and intention.

So how can we go about achieving the same? By adopting the same strategies as those famous thinkers and creators:

**Step 1:** We must orient ourselves towards employing the "intention muscle" inside our brains. That means acting and thinking in ways that keep our attentions focused on a particular idea or goal. Set aside a certain amount of time each day for the task, not letting distractions get in way.

**Step 2:** The object of our attentions should be pondered up and down, inside and out, allowing it to gain substance and momentum. Over time, the idea will emerge as something greater, like a snowball growing in size as it rolls down a hill.

**Step 3:** We need to encourage our brains to act as if they were putting together pieces of a puzzle. As the idea continues to take shape, more and more bits of data, words and symbols should be directed towards this space; we should remain focused on how they all fit together.

**Step 4:** Eventually, the initial germ of an idea will become much more tangible, perhaps marked by colors, shapes, sounds and feelings. Next, think about the books we've read, gossip we've heard and the things we've tasted and seen--basically, any experience that might relate to the topic at hand.

**Step 5:** As time progresses, it will almost seem like the idea itself is asking for more information. Meanwhile, what is needed for the idea to remain well-fed will become increasingly apparent. Soon, we will know what action will be needed to transform the idea into reality.

**Step 6:** In the end, our brains will begin to evaluate the viability as the idea firms up in shape and size. We can then figure out if it is worth pursuing or if a goal can be accomplished. Flaky ideas will fall by the wayside, while the great ones will flourish. Our brains will do their part to find those which we demand to be acted upon.

## Time to Build Your Future Wealth

Hopefully, we should all be ready to put these MGTOW character tools into action. Sleep on them first, and then use them to mold yourself into the man that you want to be. Perhaps you will be the next Tesla, Martin Luther King, Jr. or Wright brother equivalent, but the only way you can discover how to create this powerful individual is to look inside of yourself.

Discovering ourselves usually begins upon entering our college years. It is here that the most incredible experiences will become etched into our memory forever. College is the time men use to sharpen the skills required to land a great job and that super salary. We foresee a stellar career with benefits; our pot of gold at the end of the rainbow awaits. The next chapter spins a college tale for men's ears only. Meet Jayden Perkins and Brad Johnson as they prepare to depart high school. (Remember, this story is based on real events; the names and places have been changed for obvious reasons.)

⫸◆⫷

# CHAPTER 5

# The Girl Who Cried Rape

Jayden Perkins had always been the most popular girl in high school. In Clinton, Michigan, organized religion was a big deal and Jayden's father was the pastor of the United Church of Christ. The little church on Tecumseh Road was where Jayden had been baptized and it was where she expected to hold her wedding.

Teenage boys competed for her attention. Jayden would stare icily back at them because Jayden was in love with Brad Johnson: blond star quarterback, and captain of the football team.

They had slept together. To Jayden, that meant they were forever bound together. Brad and Jayden were regarded as royalty at school. The day before graduation, they strode down the hall holding hands. Jayden wore only the latest clothing and always hemmed her skirt so it barely brushed her tanned, muscled thighs.

The sea of teenagers parted like the Red Sea so that the king and queen could pass.

Jayden felt the tiny hairs on the back of her neck prickle. "I'm kind of nervous," she whispered to Brad.

"Everything is going to be fine," he said quietly into her ear. "Trust me. I'll get in." Jayden squeezed his hand.

"Congratulations, Jayden!" squealed Amanda. "I can't believe you're engaged!"

"Thank you." Jayden smiled at her friend. She noticed the way Amanda was looking at Brad. Jayden's stomach turned to stone and she snatched her hand from Brad's grasp. Brad turned to her, surprised.

"Was it Amanda?" she demanded, gazing directly into his eyes.

Brad brushed his fringe to one side. "What?"

"The girl you hooked up with. Was it Amanda?"

Brad tried to take her hand. "I told you, it was a mistake. Why can't you forget about it? She's nothing. I'm yours till the end of time, Jayden."

Her heart was beginning to melt, but she defiantly tossed her hair. Her phone beeped. She scanned the text and typed a response. As they continued moving down the hall, Jayden noticed Brad's troubled expression. "Are you okay?" she asked him.

"Well, I thought I would have heard back from the scholarship panel by now."

Jayden gave him a reassuring grin. "You're the star player. You'll definitely get it."

Tom Davis walked by, giving Brad the thumbs-up. "Brad! You is the man!"

Brad acknowledged his teammate with a casual nod. Jayden rested her head against the shoulder of Brad's letterman jacket. "It'll all work out," Brad reassured her again. He stopped walking and wrapped his muscular arms around her. He pressed his mouth against hers.

Jayden kissed him back, aware that all eyes were on them. She sank into his warmth. This was where she felt safest. Her life was about to change forever, and she would feel more ready to face the future with Brad by her side. She gazed up into his eyes. "Will you let me know as soon as you get the acceptance letter?"

"Of course," Brad replied, leaning in for their very last high school kiss.

---

In the fall, Michigan State University welcomed thirty thousand freshmen from fifty states and 114 countries. Jayden was the only one who had come from Clinton. Brad hadn't gotten the scholarship. Jayden shuffled miserably through the enrollment process before heading to her dorm room at the Betsy Barbour Residence.

She slipped a key into the lock of Room 208 and opened the door. A skinny, tattooed boy in a sweatshirt with the sleeves cut off was hunched over one of the beds, rummaging through a duffel bag. Jayden cleared her throat.

The boy turned his head and smiled, and Jayden realized he was, in fact, a pretty Latina. "Wassup?" She had even features and wore a tiny nose stud. "I'm Rinky."

"Hi! Jayden." She walked into the room and put down her suitcase. They shook hands. Rinky planted her skinny-jeans clad legs wide apart and touched a fist to her chest. On the front of her sweatshirt was the iconic image of Che Guevara.

"I believe in empowering women," Rinky declared right off. "Rebelling against the patriarchy's oppression of the female species."

Jayden blinked. "Cool. I'm from Clinton."

"I'm from Saginaw," Rinky said. "So I met this sexy biker chick on campus at last year's Take Back the Night march. Ellie. Now she's my Vin Diesel dyke. We're kicking douche-bag cave-dweller ass. Beating down the cocks and balls who run the world." She looked straight into Jayden's eyes. "Ellie's ex wanted her to die from a botched back-alley abortion."

Jayden was horrified. "Oh my God."

"Lame huh?" Rinky sat on her bed. "Ellie's just another victim of privileged white male scum," she told Jayden. "Now we're both fuckin' gender warriors in the fight for equality!"

"Equality? You want to work in the oil fields of North Dakota?"

"Huh?"

Jayden hauled the suitcase onto her bed and clicked open the lid. "Well, if you want gender equality, then you have to do all the same shit jobs they do, right?" She began to unpack.

Rinky gave her a cold stare. "I'm taking gender studies. What's your major?"

"Business. I'm going to open a flower shop back home." Jayden checked her phone. No messages.

"A flower shop?" Rinky groaned and pretended to stick her finger down her throat.

Jayden giggled. Rinky was a little weird, and Jayden had never met anyone like her before. All the same, Jayden could see the two of them becoming friends.

Rinky flopped onto her bed with an engaging smile and kept up the conversation. "The fag gestapo owns the flower industry, and that faggotted oligarchy controls Wall Street. The great white fucking way. You'll never survive, Jayden."

"Why do I feel like I'm in an episode of *Scream Queens?*" Jayden quipped.

Rinky turned pale. "TV is used by the powerful elite to sedate the working people and control their spending habits. TV sells sex by objectifying women. Fuck TV!"

Jayden's phone went off. She checked her messages. There was one from Brad.

HEY BABE. REGISTERED YET? MISS YOU.

"Aww," Jayden said. "My boyfriend texted me."

"Ah, so you're heteronormative, huh?" snorted Rinky. "Sucks for you."

Jayden shot Rinky a look. "We're engaged," she said while texting back.

YUP, ALL REGISTERED. JUST MEETING MY NEW ROOMMATE FOR THE FIRST TIME. HER NAME'S RINKY. LOVE YOU.

Jayden hit Send. "I like you. We're going to have fun."

Rinky nodded. "I like you, too. You're the type of girl who'll have an assload of pretty friends." Rinky grinned.

"Of course! I was homecoming queen at my high school."

Rinky rolled her eyes. "Well, Barbie, I'll protect you from all the perverts on campus masquerading as students. Did you know that seventy percent of college girls will be victims of gendered assault? One in four of us will be raped."

"Are you sure? Those statistics seem a bit high."

"You are right! The stats are off. Most victims don't even report it to the police. And last year, a co-ed was murdered after a big rally."

Jayden began to feel queasy. "You're scaring me."

"You should be scared," Rinky said. "The culture we live in is dominated by men who oppress us sexually. This is rape culture. Every ratchet ass with a dick and a pair of balls is out to get us."

"You're so cheerful," Jayden said.

"They found her body near Lambda Phi Epsilon—"

"Whose body?"

"That coed. Try to keep up. They found her on the pool table, naked and bloody. She'd been gang raped. And when the bastards had finished with her, they used a baseball bat to bash in her skull."

"Holy shit," breathed Jayden. "Do you mind if we talk about something else?"

"Are there Latinos in Clinton?"

"Nope. We have a black couple, though. They go to my dad's church."

Rinky rolled her eyes. "So, does your boyfriend go to this college?"

"No, he didn't get his scholarship and his parents couldn't afford to send him here."

"Scholarship? He some kind of nerd?"

Jayden laughed. "No way! He's a football player. Captain of the high school team, and a star quarterback." She sighed. "I miss him."

Her roommate scowled. "Football? You're like some poodle-skirt-wearing throwback from the Fifties!"

"What's wrong with football?" Jayden asked.

"Are you kidding me? All those knuckle-dragging goons? Shit, girl, you can smell hairy nuts and asscracks three miles upwind. Well, you'll meet plenty of ball-chucking meatheads here. Some of our juniors are NFL-bound. Marquee players. The Barbie sluts are all over them."

"Brad wanted to make it into the NFL."

"You should come to the after-game party this Saturday."

"I thought you hated football."

"I do, but who doesn't love a party? Let's go together. You can meet Ellie."

Jayden grinned. "Cool!"

"Cool."

———

A few hours later Jayden left the library, carrying a stack of books to go back to the dorm. It was dark and Rinky's horror stories looped through her mind. Jayden had the feeling she was being watched. She considered whether she ought to break into a run. Sweat was pooling under her arms. As she crossed the campus green, she spotted a dark figure lingering in the shadows up ahead. Jayden froze. The figure began to move toward her.

Jayden broke out in a cold sweat. Her throat went dry. She held her breath and tried to look unafraid. The man stepped out of the shadows. He was dark-skinned and tall with broad shoulders. "Good evening."

The man gave her a friendly wave as he passed. He headed in the direction of one of the frat houses.

Jayden sighed with relief. "Hi," she called after him.

Jayden exhaled. "I had quite a scare on my way back from the library. A black guy scared me." Her hands were trembling.

"What did he do?" Rinky said, looking alarmed.

Jayden waved a tired arm through the air. "Oh, it was nothing. I was just being paranoid. Forget I mentioned it."

Rinky bounded across the room and stood over Jayden. "What happened, girl?"

"Nothing happened, honest. He was perfectly nice."

"What did he look like?"

"He was tall." Jayden tried to remember the details of the encounter. "Oh! And he wore weird glasses. Squarish, with white frames." Then she suddenly wasn't sure whether he had been wearing glasses or she'd seen those glasses earlier in the day.

"Did he touch you?" Rinky asked.

Jayden shook her head. "No." She sat up in bed and reached for Rinky's hand. "Look, I spooked myself. Can we forget about it, please?"

"We still going to the party on Saturday? Ellie wants to meet you. I think she wants to check out her competition."

"She knows I like boys, right?"

"Ellie's kinda insecure like that."

Jayden sent Brad a quick good-night text before slipping under the covers and closing her eyes. The last thing she remembered before falling asleep was a pair of square, white glasses and the smoldering glow of the eyes behind them.

On Saturday night, Ellie came over. Jayden went into the bathroom to put on a tight pink sweater and her favorite miniskirt. When she emerged,

Ellie let out a low whistle. Rinky popped open a can of beer and handed it to Jayden.

"Fucking Barbie," Rinky said, grinning. "Knock 'em dead, girl."

They heard party music as they approached the frat house. Jayden had never seen so many people at one party. The three young women made their way towards the doorway. Students in various states of inebriation filled the steps and yard. A few of them glanced at Jayden, making her feel self-conscious. As the three girls went inside, the bass was so loud that Jayden could feel each beat reverberating inside her belly. The place stank of booze and smoke; passed-out students were strewn around the room and up the stairs.

"Let's get a beer!" Ellie shouted. The three of them pushed through the crowd towards the kitchen at the rear of the house.

Everywhere Jayden looked, people were laughing and drinking. Some were dancing, while others were making out. Jayden started to feel giddy and free. She had just finished her third beer when Ellie tapped her on the shoulder.

"You got eyes on you, Barbie girl," Ellie slurred into Jayden's ear.

"What?"

"Low-key. Big black fella over by the stereo. He's undressing you with his eyes. Has been for quite a while now." Ellie belched and gestured with a beer bottle back over her shoulder.

Jayden recognized the square glasses with the white frames. He was leaning against the wall, a beer in hand. Their eyes met. He smiled, and Jayden smiled back.

"You know that guy?" asked Rinky.

"It's the guy from the other night," Jayden shouted over the music.

"What? The freak who scared the shit outta ya? I'm gonna kick his big ass."

"It's okay. I got this. I'll be right back." Jayden began to make her way toward him.

"Hi," she said as she approached the guy.

He smiled. "We meet again." His voice was as smooth as honey. "Let's go out back where we can talk." It wasn't a question and he didn't wait for an answer. A minute later they were standing in the backyard. "I'm Rig." He held out his hand and Jayden shook it.

"Jayden," she said.

"That's a pretty name." Rig's eyes remained fixed on hers.

Jayden became aware that a group of young men and women were staring at her and Rig. They were whispering to each other.

"Can we get some privacy here, people?" Rig said.

Immediately the crowd began to disperse. "Sure. No problem, man," someone said.

"Sorry, Rig," said another.

"Fans," he said, grinning.

Jayden giggled. "Are you famous or something?"

Rig shrugged, looking embarrassed. "Kinda," he said. "I play football. I've been earmarked for the NFL. If I ever graduate, that is."

Jayden's eyes glowed with excitement.

"Hi, Jayden!" The greeting came in chorus. When she turned, Jayden saw two girls she'd met in the library. She waved at them. One minute later, two male students walked past and they also waved at her. "Hi!" Jayden returned their greeting.

"Hmm. Seems I'm not the only one with a fan base," Rig said, smiling.

Jayden blushed. She felt attracted to the football star. Just being in his presence turned her on. It was totally different from the feeling she got when she was around Brad. She felt a sudden flash of guilt.

She realized Rig was mid-flow. "Then when I was eight years old, I was just a skinny kid who loved Ka-Zar and Captain America comics. I'm from Fayette, Mississippi. It's the poorest place on earth."

Jayden flushed Brad from her mind. She wanted to kiss Rig. "I'm from an itty-bitty place myself. Clinton, Michigan. What's this music? I like it. It makes me want to dance."

"Tiesto. The best DJ around," Rig began to move his hips.

Jayden watched him. "It's hard to believe you were ever skinny."

Rig threw his head back and laughed. The sound rumbled in his chest like a distant storm. "I wasn't just thin, I was way too tall and lanky. I had these long arms and legs. I was the opposite of my comic book heroes. My self-esteem was in the gutter. I used to walk around hunched over." Rig flexed an arm. His bicep was the size of Jayden's waist. "Now look at me."

Jayden inhaled sharply. Her eyes widened as warmth radiated down into her loins. "Oh, I like," she gulped. "How did you get so big?"

"Mama's cooking. And working out for three hours a day since I was thirteen."

"Beer?" Rinky appeared, holding two cups. Ellie hovered at her shoulder. Jayden thought they both looked pretty drunk.

"Not for me, thanks. I have to play tomorrow," Rig said. "But thanks, anyway."

"Thanks." Jayden took a cup and made the introductions.

"So you're Rig Nelson?" Rinky said. "You got brains as well as brawn, big boy?"

"Well, I'm on a full ride."

"Rig's bound for the NFL," Jayden said, taking a sip of her beer. She noticed that Ellie was looking a little green. "I think you'd better take Ellie home. She doesn't look so good."

Rinky looked around at Ellie. "Fuck! I told you not to drink so much!" She took Ellie by the arm and began dragging her back toward the house. "We'll talk later," she called back over her shoulder.

"Sure!"

Jayden's heart pounded. Now she could give Rig her undivided attention. She sipped her beer and savored his words, his mouth. His body. He was like no one she'd ever met. Will Smith on steroids. She wanted him to touch her. Hell, she wanted to touch him. "You live here?" she asked.

He nodded.

"Can I see your room?"

Rig grinned. "Wow. You move fast."

Jayden smiled seductively at him. He took her by the hand and led her up the stairs.

⮜━━━

When Jayden returned to her dorm room, Rinky was still up. Rinky put down the book she'd been reading and sat up in bed. "How'd it go?"

Jayden smiled. "Ask me tomorrow. I'm still in orbit and I might be in love!"

Rinky pulled a face. "They say, once you go black, you'll never go back. He's *that* good?"

"Amazing," Jayden said in a dreamy voice. She sat on her bed, kicked off her shoes and flopped onto her bed. "Oh my God! I need to text Brad." She rummaged in her purse and pulled out her phone.

"You're going to tell him?" Rinky gasped.

"Are you crazy? I'm just going to say goodnight." Jayden typed a short message and set the phone back down on the bedside table. She stretched and yawned.

"You are one fucked-up bitch." Rinky shook her head and switched off the light.

The following Sunday at the stadium, Jayden attended Rig's game. When he came running out of the tunnel, she felt breathless. He was like a thoroughbred stallion. She almost swooned. As he ran past the crowd in the bleachers, he high-fived some of the guys. Then he leaned in and kissed an Asian girl on the lips. Jayden's gut hollowed out. Unable to move, she watched the first half of the game with her teeth clenched. Her thoughts boiled with hostility and rage. At halftime, she had to fight to keep from racing over and strangling that girl. She imagined grabbing fistfuls of her long, shiny hair and pulling it out by the roots. Throughout the second half of the game, Jayden plotted how to undermine her rival.

After the game, she waited outside the locker room, tapping a heel and anxiously adjusting her clothes. At last, the door opened and Rig appeared. Jayden's heart pounded as a pretty black girl ran into his arms. Her belly turned to ice as she watched Rig kiss the girl on the mouth.

"Hey, Rig," Jayden said softly.

Rig's eyes met hers. He looked straight through her and went back to kissing the girl.

Spots flashed in front of Jayden's eyes and reality began to sink in. She'd risked her relationship with Brad—all for a fling? What would her father think? What would Rinky think? Then Jayden's heart sank. If Brad found out, he'd be heartbroken or livid. Or both. He'd leave her for sure. As she headed back to the dorm, Jayden ran through her options. She wanted to set things right. But she had no idea of how to do that. She entered the room.

Rinky looked up from her book. "How's it going, slut?"

Jayden burst into tears and collapsed onto her bed.

"What happened?" Rinky rushed across the room. "What's wrong?" she asked, gently stroking Jayden's head.

Jayden lifted her head off the pillow. "Can you keep a secret?"

"Of course," Rinky said. "You can tell me anything."

Jayden took a deep breath. "Brad is going to kill me."

Rinky stiffened. "Oh, I know what this is about. Rig's a total player, right? Tell me he didn't fuck you over."

"This is so embarrassing. I hate his guts!" Jayden sobbed into the pillow. "I feel like such an idiot."

"How many beers did ya have at the party?"

Jayden shook her head. "I don't know."

"You're a two-beer fuck. Three, maybe."

Jayden wanted to fade away. "Don't say that! I'm not a slut! I fell for him. God! Then at the game—" Her breath hitched.

Rinky scratched her head. "So, okay. You're not a slut. But if he tells everyone you slept with him, that's what people are going to think. Everyone, all your new girl friends will slut-shame you."

Jayden didn't want to leave college in shame. She didn't want to hide in her dorm room forever. Her cheeks burned. "I'm making friends. I'm getting good grades. What can I do?"

"It wasn't your fault. I mean, after six or seven beers, you were kind of out of it, right?"

"What?"

"You'll file a rape claim," Rinky said calmly.

"Rape?"

Rinky stood up and stretched her legs. "Did he touch or kiss you without your consent? Did you verbally agree to have sex with him?"

Jayden pushed hair off her face. "No. Of course not. But—"

"You want to get out of this mess, don't you? You want to stay in college and one day marry Brad? And this guy fucked it up for you. You're nothing to him."

Jayden nodded.

"Well, now you're a rape survivor," Rinky said and bowed.

Jayden sat on her bed not speaking, not moving. A million thoughts rushed through her head.

Rinky's facial expression was as hard and cold as stone. "It's your reputation or his, girl. The college will assign a teacher or a grad student to decide the case. We'll have his fat ass in a sling. Tell him you'll file unless he forks out cash."

Jayden looked pale. "I can't *lie*. I'm a preacher's daughter."

Rinky scoffed. "Listen, you're the victim. He hurt you. You don't have to prove a thing. It'll be up to Rig to prove he didn't rape you. And you have witnesses to show you were drinking heavily that night."

"Really?"

"Do it for the sisters."

Jayden pulled her knees to her chest and wrapped her arms around her legs. She went quiet for a while.

"It's you or him, girl," Rinky said again.

"What happens if Brad finds out?"

"We'll file a private complaint. No one on campus will know it's you. Only Rig will know, and a few faculty members."

Jayden met Rinky's gaze. "Let's do it," she said.

---

The following day, two graduate students appeared at the Beta Theta Pi house with a redacted copy of the assault claim. They informed Rig of the accusation and the procedures for campus resolution. They explained the university's justice process.

Rig called his mother, who found help from an arm of the NAACP's legal services for college students. Weeks passed. Officials at the university tried to expel Rig. He was questioned by a female gender studies professor about the incident. Rig withdrew from campus life but kept all his classes and football schedules. He became depressed and angry.

Affirmative consent shifts the burden to men who've been accused of assault to prove that sex was consensual. As soon as Rig's mother secured a lawyer, the case was moved from the campus process into the state courthouse. The case made headlines in all the local papers.

Rig's defense lawyer secured phone records for the trial timeline that established Jayden's texting sequence. Jayden herself was called to testify, but she never admitted that she had consented to sex. Jayden lost the case. Rig was awarded an undisclosed sum of money in damages. He set up a mutual fund for his future. He played as the marquee-star player for MSU and was drafted into the NFL. Rig Nelson, with the help of his mother, has become a multi-millionaire and moved his entire family out of Mississippi and out of poverty.

Jayden's side of the story was believed by almost all the women on campus. The women's studies department made her a spokesperson for rape survivors and she spoke at protests. Jayden and Brad broke off their engagement, but they are still seeing one another.

## Lessons learned from Jayden Perkins and Rig Nelson

1. On co-ed campuses, female students outnumber male students. As such, they represent a huge revenue stream for the college. Admittance programs use affirmative action to enroll more women. The regents who run colleges and universities allow women's studies to define policies that help make college girls feel safe, thus attracting even more women and increasing revenue for the college.
2. Almost all claimed sexual assaults accompany drinking quantities of alcohol and/or use of other substances.
3. SHOUSE Law Group specializes in false rape claims against men.
4. Female college students who claim they were victimized by sexual assault have a myriad of emotional reasons that motivate them to concoct lies about sexual assault and file false claims.
5. The campus justice process will not penalize victims. Impunity protects women who file rape claims for various whimsical reasons.
6. Victims are assumed innocent. Their alleged aggressors are presumed guilty by campus-appointed ad-hoc judicial systems.
7. Victims are not interrogated heavily because that is called victim blaming.
8. If the female victim's parents are conservative or religious, she is likely to hold deep regrets upon waking and sobering up after a casual sexual encounter. She might convince herself that she was raped rather than face the consequences of her actions and her parents' and peers' scorn. Ambiguity about impairment levels only helps in allowing the self-convincing after a sexual encounter.

9. If the victim has a boyfriend or fiancé, her hook-up may interfere with marriage expectations and the potential for a happy future. Some women will go to great lengths to attain the goal of marriage. Some will lie.

10. A woman may file a false claim because she is interested in blackmailing the boy for his family's wealth or because he is bound for fame and fortune. Greed can be an enormous influence.

11. If the alleged assailant is a campus boyfriend who jilted her, she is likely to seek revenge. Hell hath no fury like a woman scorned.

12. Campus co-eds will sometimes lie to gain the popularity of their campus sisterhood. She will be regarded as courageous and earn a badge of honor. She will become known as an anti-rape cheerleader or advocate. She will be asked to speak about her ordeal and is likely to gain press support.

13. If she becomes jealous about anything he did or said after their intimate encounter, if she regrets her actions for whatever reason, she may be inclined to emotionally harm him. She will seek to damage his reputation in retaliation for his having damaged hers.

14. She might be a radical advocate for woman's issues, with the sole goal of manipulating situations in order to raise attention about the violent masculine behavior that she abhors.

15. Over half of campus sexual assault claims become a stand-off. Nevertheless, the most common outcome is that the male is prohibited from entering certain campus areas or he is removed from the college entirely. His future might end before it begins.

16. College men have been removed from colleges for challenging the idea of a "Rape Culture." Be wary of challenging any women's studies ideologies such as patriarchy, rape culture or the wage gap; there may be backlash.

17. Over time, colleges and universities are likely to add more sexual violence, assault and harassment policies. In Canadian universities, any unwanted attention of a sexually oriented nature, such as personal questions about one's sex life, persistent requests for a date or unwelcome remarks about someone's hair or body shape have already become taboo. So are sexist jokes.

18. Students migrate from around the world to attend US institutions of higher education. These institutions are obligated to implement politically correct policies on race, religion, gender, ethnicity, orientation and all cultural identities. These policies must cover as diverse an acceptance of humanity as possible. This maintains optimal revenue for the institution, and minimizes the risk of potential litigation.

19. Beware of co-eds who are drunk and/or high, and who exhibit aggressive sexual behavior. Contrary to popular belief, women are not always the passive parties and with a little substance like beer added in as a social lubricant, young girls often cannot govern themselves. These women are perpetrating sexual contact, but often the next day they will blame the man for a sexual assault. A woman can pose a threat to a man's future.

20. College men must be careful of all dating and hookups on campus. The law requires repeated consent, but often women will lie about whether she consented or not. Make a point of understanding all the policies regarding parties, substance use, violent actions and sexual encounters.

21. College males should go directly to the police and the legal system if a sexual assault claim is filed against them. Be prepared to fight with legal resources away from the campus courts that do not allow due process.

22. College men can file assault claims if they experience unwanted kissing, touching or if they experience or have knowledge of women who break other policy regulations. Most men would not be offended by these infractions. But men should play the game of equality by using all the rules the other side uses also.

Attending college should be the most incredible social and academic experience for everyone. Know the school's policies and play by the rules. Make your college days a remarkable and memorable time of your life. The college years comprise the most exciting, challenging and fulfilling years of a man's life. When men leave college, they can look forward to an amazing journey. Earn and save as much money as possible while you're healthy. Pay back society by contributing your skills to a cause you adore. Live in the positive and leave your mark.

With our higher education days behind us, the future is in reach and we manage the power to unlock our greatest version of us. Intention is the creator of our future. We know the dials to turn: increasing self-worth and mastering our creative ability. These levers, dials and buttons are what we can use to transport our marvelous mechanism and society towards our new dreams. It is time to pull out your MGTOW character tools to use and continue the progress by succeeding at budgeting.

⫸◆⫷

# CHAPTER 6

# Budget Your Way to More Wealth

**N**one of us likes to budget. For some MGTOW, bachelors, Herbivore men and others, we have never needed a serious budget. Now that we've examined the array of MGTOW character tools at our disposal, we can apply these towards our budgeting and wealth creation. Use your power of intention. Being frugal is the first step toward being a millionaire. Intentionally become a budgeter. Founder and former CEO of InfoSpace, Naveen Jain once said, "*Winning the football game comes from basic blocking and tackling.*" In managing our money, budgeting is basic blocking and tackling! But so many of us love to spend. Spending can be fun and exciting. People are attracted to us when we spend. Spending what we earn makes us feel free. However, you need to gain control of such emotions and take certain steps if you want to accumulate the kind of wealth that can truly liberate and empower you in the long term.

An effective, balanced budget begins with knowledge. You need to understand your spending habits and figure out which expenditures are necessary and which aren't. Do you know where your money goes each day? If not, then it's time to start keeping track with a simple diary of your daily expenditures.

To begin with, you'll need to wade through your bank statements, starting with the most recent month. Write down how much you spend on rent, utilities, food, insurance and other necessities. Move on to the credit and loans you regularly pay down. Finally, dive in and look at everything else, especially the little stuff. Don't forget to include items you purchase with a credit card or payments that are automatically deducted from your bank and other financial accounts.

Over the next several weeks and months, set aside a few moments each day to track your spending habits. That's right, make a habit of tracking your spending habits. It's best to find a time when you have a little creative energy. Some of us are morning people; others like to burn the creative juices later in the evening. Whatever the case, make sure you can remain focused on this activity; it is one that is necessary for you to achieve your financial goals.

To initiate your daily routine, place a blank sheet of paper on your desk or use the worksheet document on a computer. Then try to recall the day's purchases. Did you buy coffee, breakfast or milk for the children? Do you remember how much you had in your wallet or pocket to begin with? Did you tip someone? Ask yourself plenty of questions. You don't need to record exact amounts--you can use approximate values, when necessary--but try to avoid low-ball estimates.

The next step is to list your regular monthly payments and arrange them in order of priority. Monthly payments might be collected from your bank account. Then, based on the daily cash spending lists, you can get a monthly idea of where your money goes. Although the list will vary depending upon your individual needs and circumstances, the end result will probably look something like this:

_____***Payment to your investment fund***
_____Rent/Mortgage
_____Car Payments
_____Medical Insurance
_____Dental and Vision Insurance
_____Medications
_____Car Insurance
_____Car Gas and Maintenance
_____Car Parking, Tickets and Tolls
_____Home Insurance
_____Groceries
_____Laundry and Dry Cleaning

_____Phone
_____Gas and Electricity
_____Cable Television
_____Internet
_____Entertainment Movies, Theater
_____Entertainment Outings, Dinners, Dates
_____Credit card 1
_____Credit card 2
_____Other

# The "Pay Yourself First" Rule

You might be wondering what the top category is and why it is highlighted and bigger (***Payment to your investment fund***). Simply put, this item reflects the most important rule to remember when coming to grips with your monthly personal finances: The only way to make sure that your wealth power can grow is to ensure that you put aside enough to make it happen! Pay yourself first! Make sure some monthly money is budgeted to you. This is your savings or investment fund.

For most of us, this is not how things are normally dealt with. When we wade through the outlays, we might begin with a pile of bills and statements arranged in no particular order. Then we pay our bills. It's only *after* we've finished paying bills that we think about allocations to investment accounts. That is somewhat understandable, of course. We know that the bill collectors will soon be on our doorsteps if we fail to pay certain obligations when due. However, this often means there is not enough left over for the future.

But that sort of thinking is wrong. From now on, you'll need to list your investment account payment at the top of each month's budget. Even if it is just twenty dollars. This will ensure that when you pay what's owed, you will have secured your wealth building money, ensuring it will remain a top priority. This Pay Yourself First rule ensures that some portion of all your income will be set aside to benefit you in the future. Some use an automatic payment each month. *Set it and forget it. (For investment advice see Chapter 15 MGTOW Investing)* While many people choose to allocate as much as 10% from each paycheck, smaller amounts will still equate to a respectable investment over the course of a year.

## Why This Rule Works

At first glance, the notion of reordering your budget list doesn't seem like it would be that helpful. But there is something peculiar about humankind's monetary habits. Maybe it has something to do with our evolutionary origins, but we generally prefer a bird in the hand to two in the bush. In other words, we tend to spend what we have. It's only when we don't have the resources on hand that we curb or cut back on our consumption.

Now, though, you need to make a change: you have to be more selfish. You need to embrace the habit of thinking of your future--first of all--by making the investment-related payment a top priority. That way, once your checking account balance runs low, you will have covered all of the essentials; most or all of what you end up *not* buying will probably be optional anyway, like a jacket that goes out of style in 2 years.

One way to make sure the Pay Yourself First Rule remains effective is to arrange for the relevant amount to be automatically deducted and remitted to the financial institution where you maintain your investment accounts. *Set it and forget it!* Remember, if you can't see it, you'll find it hard to spend. Discipline yourself to have this process take place each and every month, and you'll soon find that it has become much easier to secure your financial future.

Budgeting is a lifestyle change. Aristotle said, *"We are what we repeatedly do. Excellence, then, is not an act, but a habit."*

In the next chapter we'll get creative to find a little extra cash.

⟫◆⟪

# CHAPTER 7

# Seek and You Shall Find

There is a certain magic in examining our routines. If we intentionally use our memory and creativity we might find a nugget of gold. Our mornings are full of habits and rituals that we engage in without much thought. Many of us go with whatever seems easiest just to jumpstart the day. Coffee and a sweet roll to get our hearts beating? Grabbing a morning paper on the way to work? A bagel and juice? Listening to a certain news program while in the car? Bridge toll? We probably don't even realize we're doing these things most of the time.

Because we are so caught up in our rituals, small expenditures, especially those we make in the morning, can be easy to forget. But now that you have chosen to move forward with growing your wealth, it's time to put the spotlight on even the smallest details of your financial life to see what is really going on.

The first step, of course, is to go through your spending ledger (detailed in Chapter 6), which is intended to help you take control of your finances. In a matter of weeks, you'll see just how big those small ticket items can be when you keep making them. Add them together and multiply the sum by the number of working days in a year, and you'll discover, like the mythical Greg Johnson, that you've been spending a rather large amount of money:

# Greg Johnson's List of Morning Purchases

|                     | Per day | Per year  |
|---------------------|---------|-----------|
| Newspaper           | $1.00   | $300.00   |
| Coffee              | $2.00   | $730.00   |
| Starbucks           | $3.00   | $1095.00  |
| Donuts              | $1.25   | $456.00   |
| Breakfast           | $6.00   | $2190.00  |
| Cigarettes          | $3.50   | $1277.00  |
| Beer, wine, alcohol | $3.00   | $1095.00  |
| Soda                | $ .75   | $273.00   |
| Candy               | $ .65   | $237.00   |
| Bottled water       | $1.50   | $547.00   |
|                     |         | --------- |
|                     |         | $8200.00  |

Greg Johnson spends routinely without thinking. His mind is on work or other things. Imagine if those daily purchases were your own. If so, you could save as much as $8,200.00 each and every year by eliminating them. True, some habits are close to our hearts and you probably won't be able to remove certain of them from your routine, but that doesn't mean you can't make adjustments. Ask yourself which ones are really necessary. Do you need them to survive, or are they purely habitual? Can you stop or substitute some items for cheaper alternatives?

In the case of Mr. Johnson, he decided to quit buying morning coffee, donuts and Starbucks specials and replaced those purchases with ripe oranges bought from the supermarket and instant coffee that he purchased and then brewed at home. This saved him more than $1,000.00 a month. Over time, he also stopped buying soda and candy, going with just tap water instead. The comedown from his sugar addiction was hard, but today he says that he feels better and no longer has the craving for sweets. Just as important, more money is flowing into Mr. Johnson's investment account by moving those saved dollars to his ***investment fund***, and he is beginning to look forward to a healthier financial future. It is a positive kick to see the balance growing.

Colin Powell said, *"If you're going to achieve big things, then you must develop the habits in the little things."* Have a look at your own expenditures and see if you can find ways of rethinking and transforming old patterns. Get going on making the changes and then we can start putting the savings to work for you.

Some of our best teachers are the women, men and coworkers we meet. We might even fall in love. In the next chapter we'll learn the greatest joy in life and what she means when she says *treat me right*.

⬛◆⬛

# CHAPTER 8

# That Perfect Someone

**A**s single men, many of us are socially mobile and able to meet all kinds of people as we go through life. Some of us may enjoy the freedom to meet not just one person but many. Some lift us up, while others selfishly devour our time, energy and resources. For many of us - our ability to love and our desire to be loved in return is something that defines us as human beings.

There are many kinds of love, however. While the love we receive from our parents may well be the greatest we'll ever experience, what we share with those we've selected, and who have chosen us, is the reason for our existence. What is the basis for this assumption--and assertion--that our relationships must be monogamous? And must it be forever? To believe that for every man there is only one woman whom he must remain with for the rest of his life seems more like a myopic fairy tale, more an ideal than a pathway we should all follow. Love comes in many degrees, levels and forms; is it really our lot that some are "better" than others? Most people experience serial relationships over a lifetime.

## The Special Connection

Hanging out with friends, hooking up with someone special and moving on to a dating relationship is one of the most natural and exciting progressions we can experience in our lives. Things don't necessarily have to unfold in this way, of course. The magical chemistry of attraction can strike at any time. You, me or anyone--suddenly, out of the blue, there's a moment when her eyes and our eyes meet ... and linger. *Zing!* Go the heartstrings as the emotional ripple slashes through us, our guts feeling like they are flipping upside down. Our breath catches in our throats and sparks of electricity fly. Hyperawareness draws us closer, two hearts beating as one.

In a matter of moments, the wondrous dance, the mating ritual, has begun. Suddenly, she's saying, "It's him, my one and only! At last, my prince has come!" But we see it differently. We're thinking, "Man, is she hot! It's my lucky night!" And just like that, we succumb to thinking that another carefree and unbounded relationship has just been jump-started. All that matters is that love is in the air and sex is on the menu; emotions bloom and life seems so darned good. Soon, without us even realizing, we've become an item--"a pair of lovebirds," our friends and family say. Euphoria runs deep, and every time we get together, bellies flutter and hearts race, spirits seem to merge, and talk of love is in the air. Then things get serious.

## Feelings Run Deep

At this point, it's not just love that we feel for each other. It's respect too. Our emotional and physical intimacy makes us more understanding and empathetic. Neither of us wants to hurt the other's feelings, but each of us wants to enjoy all our partner has to offer. She is our sexual partner, while we are her sexual outlet. We become increasingly addicted to each other's taste, smell and touch. The spiritual, psychological and emotional barriers that might once have distinguished and defined us seem to fall by the wayside.

But this loosening of our protective shield soon leads to insecurity. By opening ourselves up to each other, we have made ourselves vulnerable. We begin to worry about something going wrong. We fear the despair and agony of a possible breakup and heartache. We worry about what our friends and others might say behind our backs if things suddenly fall apart. In a matter of time, we begin to feel like there needs to be ground rules and boundaries to keep the relationship alive. We want to put up a united front to those around us, so we go along with demands that become more troubling over time. Directives surface about how we should behave; we agree to limits and restrictions on our actions and our friends.

Day in and day out, we continue to acquiesce, believing that we are making mutual decisions about what is and isn't acceptable within the framework of our relationship. In the name of love, we begin to lose sight of our individuality and what we want out of life. We see ourselves as a couple, constrained by monogamy. We do her bidding because we want sex; she accommodates us because of where she sees the relationship heading. We have agreed on a code to live by, designed to safeguard our relationship from outside influences and bolster it from within. No longer is it about love; now, it's a case of, 'do right by me and I'll do right by you.' We think we've created a special kind of relationship paradise. In reality, we've booked a ticket on board the Titanic, with frighteningly large icebergs ahead.

## What a Man Needs

For single men, when it comes to relationships, men don't have a lot of rules. Some guys find getting the occasional escort to be cheaper than dating, with a guaranteed outcome. We like life to be simple and uncomplicated, without drama. It is the results that matter, not the procedures, steps or phases necessary to get there. We also don't take much notice of the little things. We are more interested in the notion of a World Series home run or the possibility of a cure for Ebola than discussing, for example, whether the rooms at home need to be painted or rearranged. We dream of a day when we understand the mystery of dark energy rather than what is the best name to choose for our soon-to-be-born child or the color of the drapes in the nursery. We are natural adventurers, interested in exploring the universe for answers to great questions instead of spending lots of time and energy, like many women do, proving how terrible we men are.

That doesn't mean we don't have certain principles and requirements, of course. While they naturally vary between us, it's a good bet that many of us share at least some expectations about what we want and how we like to be treated by women. Among other things, we need her to:

1. Give us sex--however, whenever and wherever we want. If we aren't satisfied, we'll probably keep trying, but if she persists in not doing her part, we'll lose interest pretty darn fast.

2. She should maintain her looks. If not, many of us will feel the urge to find someone who does.

3. She should be sweet, kind, caring, honest, spontaneous and loyal. If she's good in bed, that might overcome some failings, but why can't we have it all?

4. She should enjoy physical intimacy with us. We want her to be interested and enthusiastic, and try new things. If not, sooner or later our primeval instincts will encourage us to go elsewhere.

5. She should be interested in us. We need women who are fascinated by and attracted to our bodies, minds, souls, passions and vocations.

6. She might encourage us in any way she can and take every opportunity to boost our ego. If not, she had better be extremely good in bed.

7. Be our companion and enjoy spending time with us, sharing experiences and adventures. But that should never be a substitute for other things, especially the intimate side of our relationship.

## What a Woman Needs

Unlike men, women have lots of rules, and we are constantly pressured to follow them. Everywhere we turn, we're expected to conform to a preset template and measure up to archaic standards created by others. Women hold all the power. In the office or on the factory floor, in the park or at a mall, at home or in church; we are ensnared in a web of sticky expectations that stifle our spirit and constrict our natural instincts. Indeed, it often seems like women have written their own wiki on the subject. Googling "how a man should treat a woman" returns a myriad of astounding results.

It seems that the *weaker sex*--pun intended--has a lot to say about what we should do and how and when we should do it.

Many of her requirements are detailed below. It's long list, but it's by no means exhaustive. If you're one of the rapidly dwindling numbers of men who still believes we have to subscribe to such expectations just to have a shot at what's inside her panties, then there's only one thing to say: read it and weep!

1. We must be polite, kind and treat her with respect at all times-- even if she doesn't deserve it.
2. We have to trust her implicitly. Even if she says or does something that isn't quite Kosher, God forbid if we question her integrity.
3. We can never lie to her. Chances are, she'll find out about it anyway and make our life hell.
4. Don't talk about exes and old girlfriends. She already hates these women, and she might use any such excuse to go out and kill them.
5. Don't look her in the eye too aggressively. Whatever you do, make sure you are the first to blink.
6. Learn to think like her. It's called reading her mind--without her knowing (yeah, right).
7. We must keep in touch with her and only her. Call, text and email her constantly; it helps her keep tabs on you. She owns you and you must never experience that special connection with any other human. She wants all your life's attention.
8. We'd better pay for everything, whether it's restaurants, movies, special events, or anything else. Don't even think about going Dutch if you know what's good for you.
9. Remember to constantly make her feel special. Buy her surprise trinkets. Leave little love notes. Tell her how wonderful she is. (You do want that bj, don't you?)
10. Remain blind when it comes to other women. You might want to think twice--or maybe a lot more--before telling her that one of her friends is really pretty. (Go on: I double-dare ya!)
11. Compliment her looks, even if it's a lie. If you find it a struggle, cross your fingers behind your back (and think bj).

12. We must listen and pay attention when she's speaking to you. Take notes. There *will* be questions afterwards.

13. Never interrupt her when she's speaking. This is not about you, silly. It's about … *um* … *eh* … what?

14. We must provide her with emotional support. Make sure you keep a pack of tissues in your pocket and that your shoulder remains dandruff-free. Trust me, she will have plenty of emotional breakdowns and we had better be there!

15. We need to learn to smell the roses. Never complain about her choice of deodorants, perfumes and other fragrances. They cost a fortune and she expects you to love them.

16. Make sure she's "in the mood." She's female and her moods swing with the moon. Keep smiling (and forget the bj).

17. Talk, talk and talk (except when you're supposed to be listening) to her. Make conversation. All the time. Even when she's quiet. She needs your attention. Always.

18. Love cats. Yes, seriously. Even if you hate the feline fur-ball beasts. Cats are cool, especially hers, her friends' and family's.

19. Show her off. Don't forget to introduce her to all your friends and colleagues with a great flourish and lots of fanfare. Bows, gestures and kowtowing is always the best.

20. Protect her (even if at the expense of your own safety). Make like you're Kevin Costner in *The Bodyguard* (bj guaranteed).

21. Tell her she's beautiful (even when she's not). Flattery will get you everywhere. But remember, never lie. Now what?

22. Understand that she's the sum of her parts. Ignore the warts and never criticize any aspect of her anatomy.

23. Stay in tune with her feelings. If she's happy, so are you. If she's sad, you're sad, too. Get it?

24. Remember: her friends are your friends (even if they look like the seven dwarves). Be happy, not grumpy.

25. There is only one answer to the question, "Does my ass look big in this?" Don't say the wrong thing. Ever! This one time you're allowed to lie.

26. Keep things clean and proper. No rude jokes, farting or picking your nose. You're not in the locker room any more.

27. Be an attentive lover, a superman in the bedroom--a man of steel. From the waist down, at least.

28. Treat her like royalty. Princesses are little girls; your woman is a queen. "On your knees, peasant!"

29. Forget your male friends and acquaintances. Say goodbye to bowling, poker nights and hanging out with the guys. Your days of fun are well and truly over.

30. Maintain a diary. Never forget her birthday, the day you met, or the first time you ever shared a Twinkie. If you do, apologize profusely and remember to write it down (if you want to avoid hell, that is).

31. Touch her, hold her hands and give her a hug. Always try to maintain some kind of physical contact (except when she doesn't want it, which you'll usually only find out after the fact).

32. Be romantic. Carve her name in trees. Bring her flowers for no reason. Plaster "selfies" of her on Facebook.

33. Call her sweetheart, hunny bunny, sweetie pie, cuddle muddle or words to that effect. If you can't think of one, there's always the Internet.

34. Invest in your relationship with her. That doesn't just mean money; it also means time, energy, emotions and showing her plenty of appreciation for being in your life. Then spend more money to prove that you mean it.

35. Never take her for granted. See that ground she walks on? You worship it, right? (Don't forget to tell her it tastes good, too).

36. Don't treat her like one of the guys, because she'll treat you like a bitch.

37. Don't raise your hand to her, even when she throws the first punch. She's female, and you must never forget it.

38. Never brush her aside. Even if she's blocking your way and shouting in your face, just stand there smiling, and wait.

39. Be chivalrous. If you don't know what that means, Google it, for crying out loud.

40. Don't fool around. Keep it in your pants, buddy, or kiss it goodbye. She will become violent, suspicious and vindictive and make your life a living hell.

41. Never order her around. Every woman wants a dominant man-- except yours.
42. Never treat her like a waitress. Store your beer on the top shelf and when you want one, get it yourself.
43. Hold the doors for her. Every door. Everywhere.
44. Trust her intuition. Don't question her when she has a certain "feeling," just be prepared for the worst.
45. Avoid sarcasm, unless it's about somebody or something she doesn't like. You'll lose, man. Women are born with sarcasm running through their veins.
46. Never challenge her authority. You're only the alpha male for as long as she's in charge.
47. Don't embarrass her in front of others, especially her friends. If you do, you'll only ever do it once.
48. Be polite and generous. Always let her have the last slice of cake, even if she could, shall we say, do without the calories.
49. Always take no for an answer. Migraines? Washing her hair? Doing her nails? "No" means no!
50. Whisper her name when you finish. For your own sake, please make sure it's hers, OK?

## Lessons Learned

While many of these "rules" seem just petty or silly, they are, in fact, unproductive and damaging to those who believe in and enforce them. They invariably create hurdles and roadblocks that lead to disappointment and failure. As the famed martial arts expert Bruce Lee once said, "*I'm not in this world to live up to your expectations.*" Or, as Canadian actor Ryan Reynolds once noted, "*When you have expectations of others, you are setting yourself up for disappointment.*" The fact is, many women have far too many expectations when it comes to men and relationships. Women wield all the power with these rules, but relationships backfire on almost all women. When women are let down they drop the man and are left paranoid and bitter. No wonder women complain they can't find a "good" man. Quite simply, no one can ever hope to measure up. The result is that most women keep getting hurt, and they remain perpetual victims; all due to strange and unobtainable expectations of what *others* should be doing.

In reality, the expectations women have are their problem, not ours. There is no such thing as the perfect someone, except in women's romance novels and chick flicks, and we should not even try to acknowledge such thinking. Besides, it is unhealthy for us to suppress our natural instincts and engage in such unnatural behavior. What's more, nowhere is it written that having one significant other is a prerequisite to lifelong happiness. Everyone is amazing in their own way, and the more connections we make, the better; they are an essential component of our genetic make-up.

This author once said, *"We must pen our own rules and take joy from wherever we find it,"* and this still holds true. The first step towards freedom is to develop an awareness of the pressures of a gynocentric world which derail our aspirations and help to transform us into self-destructive vagina worshipers. We must also be conscious of how our sexual instincts work against us, allowing money to flow from our pockets to theirs. We must be strong and independent, happy and healthy, and masters of our own destiny.

It's time to lay down the critical ground rules for ensuring our financial survival. The next chapters will examine our personal behaviors around the money we have today. Take notes.

# CHAPTER 9

# The Money Savers

**W**illiam Shatner said, *"If saving is wrong, I don't want to be right."* And guitarist Charlie Byrd said, *"A musician needs to learn to be frugal and carefully manage financial affairs."* In the last chapter, we learned about treating women right and the costs involved. We know that everyone is an individual so it is not fair to treat every woman the same, each needs personalized treatment. In this chapter we'll learn about our spending habits. But as with everything in this book, a wealth building approach works best when it is tailored to your unique circumstances. That means you need to run the gamut of your daily, weekly and monthly expenditures to get a grip on where your money is going. You don't have to fly blind, of course. A list of the spending activities and tips that others have considered can serve as a helpful roadmap for zeroing in on where the potential money savers lie. Here are just a few things you might want to think about:

1. MGTOW: Do not have children. It cost approximately $300,000.00 to raise each child to the age of eighteen (excluding college tuition fees.)
2. MGTOW: Do not marry.
3. MGTOW: Do not chase or try to impress women by buying expensive cars, extravagant dates and the latest clothing and accessories.
4. MGTOW: Reduce gift purchases on special holidays such as Valentine's Day, Flower Day and Christmas. Being with someone

and enjoying their company or a call to someone special is free and personal.

5.  Instead of buying books and magazines, why not use the resources that are freely available on the Internet.

6.  Get a library card; books, movies and CDs and even internet time are usually completely free.

7.  Watch out for regular, recurring charges from Amazon Prime and Spotify.

8.  The daily newspaper: If you can't get by without having a physical newspaper, why not share the cost of the purchase with a friend?

9.  Studies have shown that, in most cases, bottled water is not really better for you than the stuff that comes from a tap. Why not go for the latter?

10. It's no fun being cold, but it might be better for your financial future if you keep the thermostat turned down and wear layers and sweaters instead. Winter time: You might also want to consider closing off the rooms you don't use to save even more on your heating bills.

11. Social media might instigate comparisons with the Joneses, or all your friends on Facebook. This competition can be expensive and usually isn't accurate. Adjust the use of social media and become aware of any triggered enticement to buying things to "show off." Remember people are only showing their best, you are not seeing the whole picture.

12. Try to eliminate all those unhealthy pleasures and empty calories that are draining your pockets. Cigarettes, tea, soda, cigars, alcohol, candy, donuts and wine can be very costly--in more ways than one, especially over the long term.

13. It is one of life's daily staples, but coffee can be quite an expensive habit. Eliminate or cut your consumption in half. Stop going to the expensive shops--is their brand really *that* much better? Instead, stretch your budget with instant coffee and store label varieties, or maybe even switch to pure hot water.

14. Take a close look at all the other things in your life that once seemed like must-haves but are no longer necessary. Cancel the book clubs and Sports Illustrated magazine subscription and start

thinking about whether you really need to own all those high-end clothes and accessories.

15. It's hard to stop driving, especially if you need a car to get to work, but maybe you can avoid all those little side trips that cost you extra money for gas and parking. Why not ride a bike, walk or use mass transportation instead? Your car will remain roadworthy longer, your bank balance will improve and your body will almost certainly thank you for it.

16. Of course, that shouldn't be the only exercise you get. Rather than paying a monthly gym membership fee, why not work out at home, go on walks or run around in the great outdoors where you'll also inhale some fresh air in the process.

17. If you can't live without seeing those big-time sporting events, how about booking the cheap seats and inviting some friends along to enjoy the fun? It will be a blast! If you pay for NFL Sunday Ticket, share the cost by having friends over who pitch in on the fee or bring all the food.

18. Auto insurance is another expense that most of us can't do without. But that doesn't mean there's nothing you can do about. Shop around for other quotes or contact your insurance agent to see if you can prudently reduce your existing coverage, raise your deductibles or eliminate certain options, such as towing and loss of use, which you probably don't need anyway.

19. Take advantage of "affinity" and other savings programs. Many insurers, for example, have special offers available for people who don't smoke, who went to a certain school or who work for a particular organization.

20. Ask for discounts wherever you go. Just because a retailer has a price listed on that pair of pants or something else you might need to buy, that doesn't mean you can't get it cheaper, especially if you make it clear that you might have to take your business elsewhere.

21. If you need an oil change, haircut or other necessity, why not spend five minutes searching the Internet to see if you can find a coupon or special offer? Or if somebody is selling that product or service for a lower price. Craigslist might find a person like you willing to do inexpensive work to augment their income. In

situations like this, a search engine like Google can be a wealth builder's best friend.

22. Rethinking the way you handle your day-to-day banking needs can also pay dividends. You are charged a fee when you withdraw money from ATMs that are not associated with your financial institution, often by the ATM owner *and* your bank. Those small charges can really add up. If you can't use an in-network machine, try to find one with a low fee or get extra cash back with your debit card when you buy that instant coffee at the grocery store.

23. Don't forget about the other fees that banks charge. You might be able to save at least a hundred dollars or more a year by keeping a higher balance in your account than you do now. If not, maybe you should think about switching to an institution offering a better deal. You should also avoid bouncing checks or using nonessential services. Banks make a lot of money from the fees they charge; don't let them profit at your expense.

24. Telephone chargers and computers left plugged in 24 hours a day are costly. Large screen TVs use excessive power.

25. Last but not least, remember to ask questions of yourself and others. People are always finding a better deal or a way to save. Tapping the wisdom of friends, co-workers and Internet social networks can be a great way to make sure you spend less and have more!

Saving money is the beginning on your way to experiencing wealth. We should have an intentional target of $1,000 to $3,000 in savings. Once we've saved that minimum for investing in a fund we will use those savings to open our investment account. In the next chapter we'll look at ways to bring in more dollars each month toward our intended goal.

⋙•◆•⋘

# CHAPTER 10

# From Money Savers to Money Makers

**N**owadays, men are seeking a variety of ways to make what they have work better for them and to augment their longer-term aspirations. The range of potential opportunities extends well beyond fixing bad habits and engaging in frugal economies. In reality, they involve rethinking priorities, reevaluating lifestyles and reconsidering living arrangements. Apply your strength, mastery and creativity abilities. Below are just a few money makers worth considering:

1. MGTOW: Begin an investment plan.
2. MGTOW: Get a Bobcat Dozer and hire yourself out for digging jobs and snow removal.
3. MGTOW: Move in with parents or relatives, or invite them to do the same. Rent out a room to a friend, relative or non-sexual partner. Live in a recreational vehicle or communally with others in a large home, farm or apartment. Lease your garage as a personal storage or alternative parking space.
4. MGTOW: Do not marry. Do not have children or raise other people's children. Use condoms, get a vasectomy and support the use of the male birth control pill.
5. MGTOW: Buy a magnet generator and a water generator. Become a prepper.
6. MGTOW: Join the military or other organizations that may allow you to live well and save.

7.   MGTOW: Start a dog walking service for the dog lover in you.

8.   MGTOW: Buy and sell sports memorabilia or other items on eBay.

9.   MGTOW: Try to turn hobbies into cash. Consider getting involved in businesses where you can acquire or repair discarded or damaged goods and resell them for higher prices. Provide services that allow you to transform your talents into income (creative talents or skills, such as writing, computer programming, woodworking, and refinishing, house painting). Start your own small business. In most cases, you will intuitively know whether this is your destiny and will provide you with a future of wealth as well as happiness.

10.  MGTOW: Produce YouTube videos on your hobby, pets or favorite issue. Monetize them and if they are brief, funny or profound they may go viral.

11.  Prepare sandwiches to bring to work. Eat meals at home rather than dining out. Cut out junk and processed foods such as chips, crackers, soda and energy drinks. Avoid meat or choose a less expensive variety or cut. Buy in bulk if possible.

12.  Shop online or at large discount superstores. Look to purchase good quality clothing, flannel shirts, belts, hats and other accessories at thrift shops and consignment stores.

13.  Ask merchants when products will go on sale and wait for holiday and other seasonal discounts. Sign up for loyalty cards from supermarkets and other retailers that offer special savings online and in the store. Bargain with mobile telephone, Internet and cable television suppliers for "new customer" and "retention" discounts.

14.  Always use a shopping list. If it's not on the list, don't buy it.

15.  Sleep on large purchases. Before you buy, wait several days and let your mind evaluate the pros and cons (later in the book we'll discuss cybernetics). Do not purchase things for emotional reasons such as hunger, stress, anger or elation.

16.  Barter with others for goods and services.

17.  Ride a bike, walk or take public transportation to work--and anywhere else. If you must use a car, ensure that the tires are inflated and the engine is tuned, and don't speed because these habits can save money. Consider carpooling with friends.

18. Invite friends over for coffee or an inexpensive drink instead of going out on the town. Seek out and encourage the support of friends who enjoy your company and have similar interests. Take advantage of volunteer opportunities to meet new people and take part in free events and experiences.

19. Find out where the most promising and highest paying jobs are. Target those that strike the ideal balance between your lifestyle requirements and the money you can earn. Work overtime, weekends and holidays while you are young. The boom in North Dakota might be a fit for you. Consider moving to a different region, state or country for opportunities that offer solid long-term prospects. Working in Saudi Arabia and other Arab countries pays well and you'll learn first-hand what a religious monarchy is like. Then you come home with a fist full of dollars.

There is one more possible area where you can save some dollars. It is another habit. In the next chapter, we'll examine the fine art of getting high.

⟫◆⟪

# CHAPTER 11

# Too High a Cost

For some of us, getting buzzed, tipsy, inebriated, high or smashed is a reward of sorts. It can feel like the inevitable next step when we are celebrating victory or winding down after a long, hard week. Some might disapprove, but no one has the right to stop us. Even so, experience suggests that moderation in all things is generally best. Maintaining a sense of equilibrium allows our physical, emotional and intellectual selves to function at optimal levels. We often find ourselves more excited and enriched by life's journey when our constituent parts are in reasonable balance. A balanced chemistry and secure financial assets creates a natural high.

Nevertheless, it is hard to resist the urge to imbibe, inhale, ingest or participate in those things that can alter our moods and states of mind. Unfortunately, many are addictive, creating a dependence that can hurt us financially, diminish our ability to enjoy other pleasures and some also damage our bodies and minds. There are many reasons why people feel compelled to go in this direction, but only those of us who use can know what is happening deep inside. Are we running from anxiety or emotional problems? Are we angry she initiated the divorce? Are we feeling depressed or worthless? It might be better to confront these issues head on. If you can "know thyself" more clearheadedly, the universe may well be yours.

Nobody knows for certain, but it may simply be a reflection of man's ingenuity, or, perhaps, an instinctual force, that has led us to discover any number of substances and activities that can give us a lift, at least temporarily. Many of us might not even be aware of just how many of these enhancers there are, or the fact that those we might not think twice about can potentially cause a great deal of harm. Some of the more common examples are:

1.  Coffee. It is often seen as the perfect morning wake-me-up, but it might be better to go for cheaper and less addictive alternatives instead.
2.  Cigarettes. If you can break the habit, you will live longer and breathe stronger.
3.  Cigars. Save a few bucks (and maybe even have others thank you for clearing the air) by limiting your use.
4.  Chewing tobacco. It is an addiction where you have to spit ... a lot. Yuk.
5.  Sugary foods. The high from sweets, donuts and candy disappears fast, but the effects on your health may be long lasting.
6.  Sugary drinks. Many sodas, sports drinks and energy drinks contain large quantities of sweeteners. Wouldn't it be better to be healthy, get cleansed and improve your financial health by drinking water?
7.  Alcohol. Avoid drinking spirits, beer or wine when you are angry, frustrated or depressed. Cut back at meal times and your bank account will thank you for it.
8.  Gambling. Playing the ponies, wagering in the casinos and betting online can seem like a harmless diversion, but when you run out of luck, the financial losses will only add to your problems. An empty wallet might encourage alcohol use or other escapes.
9.  Marijuana. Confronting your issues head on, rather than turning to smoking weed, is the best way to reduce anxiety or stress.
10. Cocaine and Speed. Not only are they seriously addictive, they are seriously bad for your health.
11. Pain Killers: Many of us need help getting over the pain from injuries or surgery; just make sure it's only a temporary solution. These pills lead millions to heroin use and a total life breakdown.

12. LSD, Molly, Mushrooms, MDMA and other psychedelics. Quite simply, never is too often. Yet, one time can open avenues of creativity for some.

Maybe we partake in such things once in a while. Perhaps we are happy to do it more often, now that our toxic chicks and wives are out of our lives. Maybe such uppers and downers have become the crutches we fall back on or the habits we have come to ignore. Whatever the case, they all appear capable of altering our neural pathways in a way that can lead to more frequent use--the hallmark of addiction.

## Modify Your Habit

For those of us who realize that our substance use must change, the first step is figuring out what we would like to limit or stop. After all, we are the governors over everything in our lives. But it is only after we make the decision that things can happen. Use your MGTOW character tools of intention, strength and determination. That doesn't mean it will be easy. Anyone who is or has ever been hooked on a substance or activity knows how difficult it can be to end the addiction. It can help to know the right strategies or have access to the right kind of help.

One approach could be called the substitution method. Let's say you frequently use or are addicted to substance X. When you get the urge to use, try replacing some or all of the relevant enhancer with a healthier alternative. If, for example, it's Friday night when you normally consume an excessive number of cocktails, try replacing the third drink with clear, fresh water or juice. If you repeat this process each time, soon you will have established a routine that makes you feel better, and which you can feel good about. The positive reinforcement is that you've accomplished a small goal in reduction (and probably saved some money too). Mastery comes with practice.

Another similar strategy is to exchange one behavior for a better one. Instead of smoking material X and sitting and talking with friends, try something different. Hold off on lighting up and try getting up and dancing to your favorite songs instead. Alternatively, when you have the urge to ingest or imbibe, try jogging, working out, meditating or engaging in some other activity that you seriously enjoy. A simple twenty-minute walk will calm thoughts and urges. Over time, the latter will become the reward that your mind and body crave. Of course, taking the time to figure out what you like and love can make it easier to come up with a suitable alternative.

Sometimes, of course, we can't do it ourselves. Indeed, contrary to what men are often led to believe, we should never fear asking for help. That means reaching out and getting assistance from friends and family, health professionals or those who have aided other addicts in their efforts to get clean. In many cases, they can help us understand who we are and what we need, then walk us through the darkest places in our mind to find the light.

We may have to eliminate a friend if they use with us. Friends are the best thing in the world unless they use any substance heavily. When they do, it always influences our behavior in a negative way.

## The Single Life is Wonderful

Life as a bachelor can be filled with incredible times, but it's important that we cherish and remain good to ourselves. Good health leads to wealth. Preserving our physical form and soothing our souls as we travel down life's highway can offer its own rewards, but so can having a well-oiled, content and peak-performing machine that others appreciate. Developing money management and investing habits will return rewards that a habitual substance use cannot. Yes, we all have weaknesses, limits and bumps; but ultimately, everything that is us, both inside and out, is perfect. However, even the amazing requires nurturing.

Have you wanted to own a home or has someone told you that you should? The next chapter looks into your sense of lifestyle in hopes of answering that question for yourself.

⋙◆⋘

# CHAPTER 12

# A Future in Real Estate?

There was a time when wise elders and advisors recommended to upwardly-mobile adults that they consider owning a home. A personal residence was viewed as a safe asset that would appreciate in value as lives progressed and children grew older. Once the nest was empty, its owners could ease into retirement and live out their days in peace and idle comfort. For many people, a home in the suburbs was truly the American dream, a safe and happy place to raise a family.

But times have changed. Aside from a sudden appreciation of the risks of owning property, not everyone wants the once iconic dream of marriage, children and two cars in the garage. And millions of marriages end. Not everyone is looking forward to a grandfatherly existence with a lifelong partner. For confirmed bachelors and young MGTOW, the immediate focus is likely to be "needs first" and not worrying about diving into home ownership. If you live with your parents, for instance, it might be worth staying put until you've saved a sufficient sum. The reality is, unless you have a wife and children already, you have many options open to you. You can use what you have to establish residential permanence or purchase a life of freedom, or choose from among the variations in-between.

# Renting vs. Owning

For many people, **renting** a home offers considerable benefits. When somebody else owns the roof over your head; the insurance costs, property taxes and maintenance charges fall on them. You'll never have to fix a hole in the ceiling, repair tiles in the bathroom or repaint the exterior, and the headaches that can crop up at all hours of the day or night are not your problem.

As a renter your free time remains yours to do with as you please. Men love hobbies and sports. As a renter you may find more time to dedicate to a hobby or even a side business. You certainly can watch all the games you want to on a Sunday afternoon.

In addition, renters often enjoy the best locations in many cities and towns, enabling them to thrive in style. While it might be impossible to buy a Fifth Avenue coop near New York's Central Park, you can probably find a rental there. Then there's the flexibility that such a set-up affords you: you can go live in the Mojave Desert one year, the Swiss Alps the next.

Renting is not for everybody, of course; some men crave **ownership** at the expense of greater freedom and mobility. For them, having a place they can call their own is rewarding in its own right. It provides a sense of grounded permanence that can be quite reassuring. You'll know, and others will too, just where you are and where you'll likely be for the foreseeable future. But ownership brings numerous burdens and responsibilities with it. Aside from such routine expenses as insurance, maintenance and taxes, you'll also be faced with one-off repairs, unavoidable upgrades and pressure to maintain common areas. Not everyone will mind, of course. For those who like to putter and tinker, and have a certain knack and skill; fixing and rebuilding is something to look forward to. That person might be you.

But these aspects are only the half of it. Unless you inherited your home or were lucky enough to buy it for cash, you will invariably have a partner in the deal: the bank. Regardless of what it says on the title, the lender owns the property and you have to make the payments, often over many years, to ensure you can stay there. You are a debtor, plain and simple, and you are beholden to the entity that lent you the money. If you fail to make your payments on time, your credit record is dinged and you could find all the money you invested in the home has just vanished.

Men often have a short-term disability that prevents regular work. This can easily cause a missed mortgage payment. If you miss enough of them, your lender will step up the pressure, and maybe even take steps to kick you out. Being able to meet this obligation each month demands a consistent income. You won't be able to take time off, even if an injury or medical problem takes you out of the workforce for a while. If you suddenly fall in love and want to fly off to France with your newfound love and spend three months biking through the countryside, you'll find the lender will be less than accommodative.

## Owning for Minimalists

There is a new explosion of 'Tiny Homes' that are for sale and can be a very exciting way to live for some. Tiny homes are the new cheap bachelor pads! As a single guy, they are an attractive alternative, and they very much fit into the MGTOW philosophy. While many think of tiny homes as cheap and unbearably small, many tiny home designs are actually spacious and very cozy! Many MGTOW don't need much for a home in size and these tiny homes are constructed in quaint styles with elegant finishing touches. Plus they are inexpensive.

Some might want to live in a mobile home at a trailer park. Others might enjoy living and traveling the roads in a RV recreational vehicle.

## Investing in Rental Properties

For some men, owning a home is not enough; they want the financial and other benefits that can accrue from owning rental properties, often financed with other people's money. On the face of it, the arrangement sounds great. You purchase an apartment, office building or warehouse, and use the money that tenants pay you to cover the financing and operating expenses. Over time, the property rises in value and your equity increases, leaving you with a large nest egg after a number of years. It sounds like a simple money making plan, a sound business opportunity.

Other men buy properties with the intention of fixing them up and flipping them back to the market to sell for enough to cover all costs plus a profit. This is risky unless you are part of a group of friends who are experts at all the fixing that will be needed.

Unfortunately, the reality of flipping or owning income property can be quite different than envisioned. Experienced owners will tell you that rental property ownership is often a never-ending headache. For one thing, tenants come and go. Finding and screening them can take time, and it is easy to be fooled by those who seem forthright but who are actually psychopaths in disguise. When they leave, you may have to repair and refurbish the property and allocate additional time and money to lining up replacements, without having any income coming in to cover the costs. Some rental units can stay unrented for six months out of a year.

Worse still, if you are stuck with bad tenants who complain endlessly or who otherwise decide not to honor their obligations, your part-time investment can turn into a full-time nightmare of legal fees and court appearances. Owners often become attached, to a certain extent, to their tenants. When an owner's renters have problems such as a renter's illness, divorce or missed work the owner is often emotionally burdened as well, sometimes the owner realizes the renter has children and feels too guilty to demand rent if the parents give some excuse, therefore rent goes unpaid. None of this takes account of the hoops you have to jump through to satisfy government rules and regulations.

In the end, the decision about whether to buy and what to own comes down to who you are as an individual. Take pains to understand yourself inside and out before taking the plunge. For a long time, the idea of owning a direct stake in the place where you live was a middle class myth that few people challenged. But we all have different wants and needs. Some men love their day job or hobby, while others marry their work and leisure interests. Only you know what you have to offer and where you want to devote your time and energies in the decades to come.

It is time to plan for your future.

———◇———

# CHAPTER 13

# Planning for More

So far on your personal finances we've covered the rules for saving and making more money, with the topic of getting high and real estate investing thrown in for good measure. We've learned about habits and how to change them. We've also talked about problem solving and the power of intention. The next step is to integrate those rules into a broader plan of action for growing your wealth, which can be loosely set forth as follows:

## Grow-Your-Wealth-Plan

1. Live within the constraints of your budget.
2. Limit your use of credit.
3. Purchase assets that can compound or grow in value over time.

Needless to say, this simple approach is at odds with what we've long been told. Even today, despite the many economic upheavals the world has seen in recent decades, we are encouraged to disregard such practical and prudent measures and instead, to squander money on goods and services we may not need, like fancy cars, luxury apparel and expensive vacations; to rely on credit to acquire those things we can't really afford. It is a topsy-turvy world where debt is not the prison that limits our choices and money is seen as something other than powerful.

Arguably, we could all end up with more if we simply stuck with the grow-your-wealth plan. Instead, many of us have preferred to keep up with the Joneses, paying through the nose for the myth of the American Dream. Many have not taken the time to study and differentiate between real wealth and the illusion that we can keep acquiring things that are beyond our means. Some invested in college and certifications. Others bought the motorbike, snowmobile and camper. Instead of breaking our backs to repay lenders for unnecessary luxuries, we could have been accumulating the assets that would be working for us instead.

## The Path to Financial Despair

The mantras of the borrow-and-spend consumption culture aren't the only false promises that have put men's economic wellbeing at risk. We also live in a society that has placed romance and love on the highest pedestal, making it a priority above all else. For men, relationships are expensive. After graduating from high school or college, the traditional journey has been to follow the path of Tom Carlson, a close friend of the author, who saw his adult life begin with love and, sadly, end in despair.

Indeed, before Tom Carlson even reached the age of 30, Tom's life had been spinning out of control for years. Below is a quick snapshot of where things stood less than a decade after he had received his college diploma:

- He accumulated $15,000 in school loans.
- He financed the purchase of a new car, a Lexus ES, for $37,000, to impress women.
- He purchased, on credit, $7,000 in new clothes and shoes.
- He dated, wined and dined a number of women, charging all of it to his many credit cards.
- He fell in love with Shirley and, within a year, had asked her to marry him. He then spent $9,000 in borrowed money to buy her an engagement ring and pay for their wedding.
- He fathered a baby boy, which led to several thousand dollars of related expenses, many of which were not covered by insurance.

- He purchased a home and a car for his wife and child, taking on a mortgage and another auto loan in the process.
- He fathered a newborn daughter, doubling the family's child-related expenses.

In sum, Tom accumulated more than two million dollars in debt, not counting all of the interest he will have to pay on the balances. The debt was an emotional burden and he was determined to be a man and keep providing it all. Shirley, his wife, was fulfilled with a husband, baby and home. Consequently, Tom earned 60K a year but he had to get a second job that he disliked so he could keep up with all the bills. He will have to spend the next 30 years on a treadmill just too barely hang on to what he's got. Because of his huge debt load, his freedom is severely limited, things are tense at home, and he regularly needs a drink to dull his stress and pain.

Tom Carlson also feels like the family pack mule. He can't find relief. His wife complains and nags when money is tight. She spends the family money for what she labels the family needs. Tom is worn down in the process, and he feels despondent and occasionally even suicidal. He has become yet another man who fell in love without understanding the costs and financial burden, therefore he found himself becoming a prisoner to work and his family. He is also one of the estimated one-in-ten males that point to their spouse and/or family as a frequent source of excess demands and worries.

Tom's burdens and everyday responsibilities overwhelm him financially, physically and psychologically. This isn't the only thing he has to worry about. With each passing year, the children are growing up and it appears that conditions have reached a point where it is likely that his wife, Shirley, will decide he is not good enough and join the many other women who have divorced their husbands, potentially saddling him with the added expense of alimony and child support payments, along with limited or even no custody rights to his children.

Hopefully, you are one of the enlightened few who have not fallen for the alluring trap of love, sexual relationships or family. While the pursuit of marital bliss is something our society sees as a time-honored tradition, it is, more often than not, the pathway to a hellish life, or even a slow death, for most men. We should be allowed to love, but without having to pay with our last drop of life-blood. Regardless of whether you are open to loving someone or not, it is time to start thinking differently about how, why and where you spend your money. Debt is a serious bummer and we can all look forward to an upper by tackling debt head-on.

The next chapter is about bailing yourself out of debt, and it is going to be tough. Debt is the American way. Each of us needs to do our best.

# CHAPTER 14

# Out of the Hole

In the last chapter, we discussed the perils of borrowing money and using credit cards. But having more debt than you can afford to pay back is a problem whether you are on your own or in a relationship. For one thing, when you are in hock, you are granting your lenders a measure of control over your life. All the benefits of being single and ready for action can fade away or be taken from you when you are beholden to banks and other big money interests.

What's more, surviving on borrowed money and amassing large amounts of debt can be addictive and harmful, potentially setting you up for the sorts of bad endings that drugs, gambling and other "highs" can bring. The situation is even worse when interest rates are high or when lenders can raise them at will. Some credit cards charge 24% interest or more. Even if you have an investment earning 8% income, you are paying far too much on that 24% credit card to remake anything from the 8% investment fund. If you can only afford to pay the minimum amount due each month, you could easily find yourself trapped in a debt spiral-- lumbering with an endless cycle of payments and enslaved to your creditors for life.

The risks of being weighed down by amounts that might not seem all that large at first become clearer when you dig down and do the math. Did you know that if you owe $10,000 on your credit cards, a position that even some recent college graduates find themselves in, it will take you more than **35 years** to eliminate that obligation if you only pay the **minimum** amount due each month? Instead of using your money to grow your wealth, you'll be paying lots of interest and ensuring your lender grows his instead! Sadly, that is where they want you to be, but it's not where you belong.

Needless to say, the burden of borrowing can have a major impact on your mental and physical wellbeing. When you are struggling to stay afloat, you feel like you are shackled and suffocating, your self-esteem draining by the day. The constant pressure can create considerable stress and place added wear and tear on your spiritual *and physical* health. Over time, it can lead to all sorts of ailments, including high blood pressure, difficulties concentrating, indigestion and other stomach problems, not to mention a lack of sleep. Credit cards are like a nagging wife who's constantly complaining and shouting at you: "time to pay up!"

If you aren't already in this predicament, then the solution is easy: budget wisely, live within your means, ensure that your investment account remains at the top of your list of expenditures, then enjoy all that you have. However, if you are unfortunate enough to have taken on a great deal of debt, then it's time to focus on two things: ending the addiction to borrowed money and getting your financial house in order. Among the steps you'll need to take:

1. Stop using your cards and cancel or cut up all but a few. This is the most painful part, but also the most necessary. You need to refrain from doing the thing that got you into the position you are in now. Certainly, it is hard to function without plastic in a wired world, but you need to see credit cards for what they are: a convenient tool, not a dangerous crutch.

2. Rethink your spending habits. Figure out what you really need and what you can actually afford. If you don't have the cash to buy a new suit or go on vacation to some faraway place, this means only one thing: don't do it.

3. Figure out what you owe and to whom, as well as what you can afford to pay down each month. There's no point in creating a plan of action if you don't have an accurate roadmap to follow. Make

use of helpful resources, including debt calculators and budgeting programs which are freely available online.

4.  Pay off the debts with the highest interest rates first. While it might seem tempting to get rid of the smaller, less costly obligations in the name of simplicity, you will likely be worse off in the grand scheme of things.

5.  Avoid quick fixes, consolidations and so-called "solutions." Lenders and shady operators may offer you the opportunity to stretch out your payments or combine your loans into one longer-term obligation with smaller monthly payments. Unfortunately, you'll end up paying a lot more in interest than now, and if you lose your job or something else goes wrong in the near term, you're prospects will be even bleaker.

6.  Don't make the mistake of paying your bills late or with bad checks. The extra headaches you'll face and the exorbitant fees you'll be charged will only add to your woes.

7.  Debt can become a habit when we purchase things using credit or payments. Replace the need to purchase with another exciting activity. Instead of buying on the credit card, take a walk, jog or workout. Make it fun and rewarding to suppress credit purchases.

Depending on how difficult things are, you may feel overwhelmed at first, believing there is no way you'll be able to dig yourself out of the hole you're in. But once you begin, success will feed on itself and, over time, you'll see the fruits of your efforts. Your monthly payments will fall, the interest and principal you owe will decline, the amount of money you are left with each month will increase … and your outlook will improve. Eventually, you'll achieve your goal and be ready for the next step of growing your wealth.

The time has come to devote attention to the most important person in the universe.

⟫◆⟪

# CHAPTER 15

# MGTOW Investing

**M**any MGTOW, bachelors, Herbivore men and others have discovered the thrill of being free from the financial enslavement associated with having a wife and family. They know the joys of having extra money in their pockets for hobbies and other luxuries. But not all of that cash should be spent today; some should also be saved to build wealth for tomorrow. Even if you have children and an ex-wife, your financial circumstances can be improved by taking some portion of what you have now and investing it.

For the layperson, learning about and understanding the process of managing one's finances can seem daunting. The world of economics, finance and investment is broad and complex, replete with buzzwords, terms, processes and laws that may require a degree or years of experience to fully comprehend. There are schemes and scams out there too, which can undermine your financial wellbeing if you fall into their trap.

One thing this approach is definitely *not* is a get-rich-quick scheme. This approach avoids bad and high-risk investments like hedge funds. It is also not gambling, day trading, storing bags of gold or silver in the basement, investing in a family member's business idea or piling into real estate. As Tom Leykis has often said on his eponymous radio show, "A *man's value grows as he ages.*" So, too, can a man's assets if he has a time-tested strategy in place. The sooner you begin, the more your money can compound. Over time, you'll be amazed at how much and how fast it grows.

Fortunately, there is a relatively simple way to do this. It is a conservative, tried-and-true method, neither too involved nor too risky, for growing your wealth over time. The strategy detailed in the pages that follow represents a simple, focused and conservative roadmap for a journey you'll be grateful you began. In a year or so, you will likely be better off financially, with more confidence and greater self-esteem than now. Over time, your success might even inspire you to take matters to a higher level, setting the stage for a potential transition to genuine tycoon.

Not everyone fully understands the payoff from thinking about and preparing for the future, so it's a message that bears repeating: *no matter your age, putting money aside for a rainy day or retirement is a sound survival strategy.* This book will help you grasp the instruments and approaches that will serve as the foundations for a better financial life. Once you understand the mechanics and start taking the necessary steps yourself, you'll find you are truly the master of your financial destiny.

## Now is the Time

To begin your journey, you will need a seed pot of savings that you can use to put your long-term investment plan into action. Although the amount will vary depending on your individual needs and circumstances, a minimum of $1,000 to $3,000 is probably ideal. Once this money is moved to your investment accounts, you will be on your way to growing your wealth without having to expend a great deal of additional effort.

Of course, you will need to keep tabs on your investments, as you should always do in any area of your financial life, to ensure that your money is working for you. You will also have to learn some key terms and certain details about markets, the intermediaries you will be doing business with and the kinds of investments you will own, so that you understand what you are doing and why. That doesn't mean you will be diving deep into the world of high finance, or spending days or weeks toiling with textbooks or attending classes, though you certainly can if that interests you. The emphasis in this case is on simplicity and straightforwardness.

Once you go down this path, you'll find that it will change your life and become an important component for increasing your wealth-building potential. Perhaps it will do more than that. You might find the topic of investing engaging and seek to learn more. While the basics of money-building are relatively straightforward, there's a vast trove of academic and other resources about finance and investment strategies available. The goal here is simpler: it is intended to help you feel confident that you have and know what it takes to move forward.

Whatever the case, make sure that the study of your finances becomes a weekly habit. Success comes from altering a few behaviors, they become daily habits. In many respects, we are living in the best times possible for creating wealth, as the Internet affords even the smallest investors the opportunity, ability and resources to achieve financial independence. By directing your attentions in this way, you are exercising a financial muscle that can only grow stronger. Certainly, there is a steep learning curve involved, as there are in many areas of life. However, taking the time to learn and understand this particular subject will empower you and help to ensure a future of financial freedom.

———⟫◆⟪———

# CHAPTER 16

# A World of Markets

Every day, people around the world buy and sell a mind-boggling array of goods, services, promises and securities, including stocks, bonds, commodities and investment funds, either through direct communications with one another or via centralized marketplaces such as stock exchanges. The trading can be fast-paced and hard to monitor amid volatile conditions or changing volumes.

One way that those who care keep tabs on broader price trends is by monitoring indexes whose values are calculated based on the prices of the items being bought and sold in a particular trading arena. We often hear investors ask, for example, "What is happening in the stock market?" Generally speaking, if the value of a particular stock index is moving higher, the price of most, if not all, of the securities it is based on are increasing in value.

So, what kinds of financial instruments should those who want to grow their wealth be concerned with? In reality, even most experts would find it hard to list the full range of possibilities. But historically, investors have tended to focus on equities, which are also known as common stocks or shares. For one thing, publicly traded shares, which can be freely bought and sold by anybody, represent stakes in organizations that play a key role in the economy. When a company is making money and doing well, investors tend to value its shares more highly; when many firms are doing well, so, too, does the overall market.

In the U.S., the shares of the largest businesses trade on the New York Stock Exchange (NYSE) and the NASDAQ Stock Market (NASDAQ). If you watch a financial news channel like *CNBC*, for example, you'll notice that companies are often referenced by a symbol comprised of a small number of letters. These are assigned by exchanges to make it easier for people to identify, trade and learn more about them. One such example is "WMT," which is the symbol for America's largest bricks-and-mortar retailer, *Wal-Mart Stores Inc.* Most other securities also have symbols associated with them for the same reasons. Generally speaking, it is not necessary to memorize the symbols as they can easily be found in newspapers and online.

When people want to know how the broad equity markets are doing, they tend to focus on certain benchmark indexes whose prices rise and fall based on transaction prices in the underlying shares. The most popular varieties are those that happen to have been around a long time and which have been monitored by investors throughout the world for decades. Below we will look at three of them.

## Measuring the American Markets

| | | | |
|---|---|---|---|
| **DOW** | 17755.08 | +11.76 | +0.07% |
| **NASDAC** | 5074.274 | -21.42 | -0.32% |
| **S&P 500** | 2088.87 | + 1.21 | +0.06% |

- Dow Jones Industrial Average (DJIA), or Dow, which is a price-weighted average of the prices of the shares of 30 of the biggest and most well-known companies in America, many of which are also referred to as blue chips. The DJIA was invented by Charles Dow back in 1896.
- NASDAQ Composite, which is a market-capitalization weighted index of more than 3,000 common stocks and similar securities listed on the NASDAQ. This index includes the world's foremost

technology and biotechnology giants, such as Apple, Google, Microsoft, Oracle, Amazon, Intel and Amgen.

- Standard & Poor's 500, or S&P 500, which is based on the market capitalizations of 500 large companies having common stock listed on the NYSE or NASDAQ. The constituents of the index and their weightings are determined by S&P Dow Jones Indices.

Although the U.S. is the focus of this book, other countries also have actively-traded equity markets where some of the largest companies in the world, including Royal Dutch Shell, Toyota, Honda, Samsung Electronics and Daimler, have their shares listed. Among the more well-known benchmarks are Canada's TSX Composite, Japan's Nikkei Stock Average, Germany's DAX and the United Kingdom's FTSE-100. Those who are in a position to do so may find these markets worth exploring somewhere down the road.

## International Markets

### Canada
TSX Composite Index
### Asia
Nikkei Stock Average
Shanghai Composite Index
Shenzhen index
### Europe
United Kingdom FTSE
German DAX
France CAC 40

Once you've started investing in earnest, the various indexes can serve as guideposts that can help you to quickly and easily keep tabs on how your own investments are doing. Certainly, it has often been said that the stock market is actually a market of stocks, meaning that some companies' shares will invariably outperform others' because their businesses are faring better. Over the longer term, however, the prices of most stocks tend to rise when indexes are trending higher, while the opposite holds true when indexes are falling.

It's worth repeating, of course, that prices rise *and* fall. In fact, the one thing you can say for certain is that things will change. No matter where markets are now, they will likely be different in a month, a year, or a decade. And, as we saw after the dot-com bubble burst in 2000 or when the global financial crisis erupted in 2008, sometimes they can suffer dramatic falls, even over a matter of weeks.

History suggests, however, that the long-term trend for share prices is up, and that significant declines in prices, however painful they may be at the time, tend to be temporary. Nobody knows for sure how things will turn out in the future, but panic selling after big drops has generally not been the best of decisions. Hence, the better bet has been to stick with a disciplined, long-term investing approach. The reality of it is that stocks rise and drop. Sometimes markets correct. Sometimes a global financial crisis hits. The key here though is to not only *not* sell on panic, but also to be diversified enough and strong enough by investing in funds that will weather the storm.

———◆———

# CHAPTER 17

# Choosing a (Financial) Partner

In most countries, individuals would find it difficult, maybe even impossible, to buy or sell stocks or other securities without using a "middle man" such as a brokerage firm. In theory, this arrangement is supposed to be for the benefit of investors, helping them to avoid being taken advantage of and to achieve their goals without too much hassle; in reality, brokers make money on everything you do and, unfortunately, they don't always look after your interests.

It is possible to invest in a limited range of financial instruments, most notably mutual funds, by establishing a relationship with an institution, like Vanguard or Fidelity, which issues and markets such investments.

Once you have decided to move forward, you will need to find a firm you feel comfortable with. As with every financial relationship in your life, you must weigh up any number of variables, including costs, technology, convenience, reputation, etc. Some of you might want to deal with a live person by visiting an office or calling someone on the phone. Others might prefer going online, where you can open an account and invest with the click of a mouse (or, perhaps, a few of them). Online, you can formulate a question and email it in and usually get an informative response back within 24 hours.

Whichever intermediary you choose, you will have to provide them with a great deal of information about you and your financial goals, including, if you are in the U.S., a social security number. Banks and brokerages in most countries worldwide are required to "know their customers" because of rules that are designed to prevent money laundering and other financial crimes.

# Worldwide Investment Partners

### America
Vanguard (www.Vanguard.com)
Charles Schwab (www.schwab.com)

### Canada
Questrade of Canada (www.questrade.com/smart-etfs)

### Asia
Boom Securities Hong Kong (www.boom.com)
Philip Securities Hong Kong (www.poems.com.hk/zh-hk)

### Europe
TD Direct Investing UK (www.tddirectinvesting.co.uk)
Barclays Stock Brokers UK (www.barclaysstockbrokers.co.uk)

In general, there are two kinds of accounts available in the U.S.: taxable and tax-deferred. The former are like any other financial account, in that if you make money, you have to pay taxes, and if you lose, you may be able to reduce what you owe. Examples of the latter include individual retirement accounts, or IRAs, which allow you to save and compound money without paying taxes until you actually withdraw the proceeds at some future date, typically after retirement. Many businesses also provide similar options for their employees known as 401(k) plans (named after a section of the federal tax code).

Once your account has been approved and set up, you will need to make a deposit or arrange to transfer funds from your bank or other financial institution to the brokerage firm so that you can begin investing. The amount you will need to get started will vary by institution; in some cases it can be as low as $500.

# Getting Down to Business

Although there are a variety of ways in which you can allocate the money that is in your account, initially at least, many people invest it in a money market fund. Generally speaking, money market funds are like mutual funds and exchange traded funds, the latter of which will be defined shortly, in that they all allow multiple investors to take a stake in a pool or basket of securities or other assets.

Traditionally, money market funds might hold investments in certain types of securities issued by governments or banks, for example, which originally sold them to raise money for various purposes. Typically, these kinds of funds are viewed as relatively safe investments; they generally don't rise and fall in value in the same way that other investments do, though, as with all securities, there is always a risk that prices might fluctuate over time.

Some varieties of pooled investments, like mutual funds that hold portfolios of stocks, can be much more volatile, because their value, like that of the various stock indexes, is affected by what happens to the prices of the underlying securities. If a mutual fund owns all the stocks in the S&P 500, for example, the value of a stake in that fund, including your own, will tend to rise and fall with the index.

Normally, you can only acquire or dispose of mutual fund shares once per day, usually prior to a cut-off time determined by the brokerage firm or entity that "sponsors," or created, the fund. The alternative is to invest in an exchange-traded fund, or ETF, which you can buy or sell anytime during market trading hours. Simply put, an ETF is a tradable security that represents an ownership interest in a portfolio of stocks, bonds, commodities or other assets, typically agreed to before it was brought to market.

# Keeping an Eye on Costs

One very important consideration when investing in any security or fund are the costs and fees involved. When you buy or sell a stock or an ETF you will typically pay a commission to the firm that handled the transaction, which increases your costs or reduces your proceeds, respectively. In addition, many mutual funds and ETFs compensate brokers and/or the firms that issue them by including fees that are factored into the price. If you buy a mutual fund with a "load," for example, there is a hefty commission included in the upfront charge; if it is a no load fund, there isn't.

In general, it is best to favor investments that have low expense ratios, which means more of your money is being put to work and less is being used to pay somebody else for the privilege of having it. While the amounts can vary depending upon the nature of the underlying investments, the sum of money involved, and the type of financial institution you are dealing with, opting for investments with expense ratios that are below 1% per year is probably a good rule of thumb.

It's worth bearing in mind, of course, that it is difficult to invest without relying on others. Still, including financial partners, nobody will assume responsibility for your success. Remember, in the end, it's your money, not theirs.

<hr />

# CHAPTER 18

# The Right Target

Now that you have opened an account and have deposited money into it, the next step is to choose where and how you want to invest. As noted earlier, there is a dizzying array of possibilities, which can be confusing to even the most knowledgeable investors. It is easy to listen to what people say and get confused. But as in many areas of life, it is generally best to narrow the focus and remain diversified. While nobody knows for certain which investments will outperform others or where the biggest treats are, it can help if you try to minimize certain types of them.

It is unwise to purchase a bunch of company stocks because it is hard to manage a portfolio comprised of the shares of a great many companies, as you probably won't be as knowledgeable about the ups and downs of their various businesses as a full-time investment professional would. It is also easier to get sucked into chasing performance, where you jack up your investment in a particular stock because it is doing well--until it doesn't. Having so many different securities to watch can be stressful and time-consuming. And making many trades on individual company stocks will spend your money fast in fees! So this approach is not suggested.

## Two Factors, Two Types of Funds

Two types of investments that allow you to take the least amount of risk factors into account are sector specific mutual funds and ETFs.

Typically, these securities represent stakes in shares of companies that do business in somewhat comparable industries. No two firms are exactly alike, of course, but a company like Exxon generally has to deal with the same issues as Chevron. Under the circumstances, you probably wouldn't be surprised to hear that both are included in an energy sector ETF. The same goes for health care, for instance, or financial companies.

Of course, things are not quite that simple. While there are broad-based energy funds, for instance, there are also more narrowly-defined varieties, including funds that invest in oil drilling, gas pipelines or gasoline refining companies. But again, it is generally best to stick with the K.I.S.S. rule: "Keep it simple, stupid!" This should not be taken as an insult, but rather as advice worth following. For the most part, all publicly traded stocks are categorized as belonging to one of the following 10 sectors:

1. Consumer Discretionary. Examples include retailers, media companies, apparel makers and automobile manufacturers.
2. Consumer Staples. Food, beverage, tobacco and household product makers.
3. Energy. Energy exploration companies, oil and gas drillers and integrated power firms.
4. Financials. Banks, insurance companies and real estate firms.
5. Health Care. Hospital management firms, health maintenance organizations and pharmaceutical manufacturers.
6. Industrials. Aerospace and defense firms, machinery manufacturers, toolmakers and construction equipment producers.
7. Information Technology. Electronics producers, computer manufacturers and software makers.
8. Materials. Mining companies, chemical producers and forestry product manufacturers.
9. Telecommunication Services. Wireless operators, cable companies and Internet service providers.
10. Utilities. Electric, gas and water suppliers.

Real world examples make it even easier to understand. Among the sector specific exchange-traded funds sponsored by Vanguard, for example, are the following (more detailed information can be found at their website):

1. Vanguard Consumer Discretionary ETF (symbol is VCR). Holdings include shares in Amazon, Comcast, Home Depot, McDonald's, Starbucks and Nike.
2. Vanguard Energy ETF (VDE). Exxon, Chevron, Conoco, Schlumberger, Phillips 66 and Kinder Morgan.
3. Vanguard Information Technology ETF (VGT). Apple, Alphabet (formerly known as Google), Microsoft and Facebook.

Of course, determining which sectors you should invest in, and how much, depends on any number of things, including your own knowledge and experience. A famous money manager, Peter Lynch, has often said, *"Investment success comes from focusing on what you know best."* If you are a technology geek, you may base the decision on whether or not to buy or sell an information technology fund on your own personal experience. A doctor might do the same when it comes to health care funds.

Alternatively, if you like to keep close tabs on what is happening in the business world, and are knowledgeable about which industries tend to fare best at certain points in an economic cycle, you might want to use this knowledge to guide your decisions. If you sense that economic conditions are becoming more difficult, for example, you might want to steer funds away from the consumer discretionary sector ETF and shift them to the consumer staples ETF instead. You can then reassess and rebalance holdings as circumstances change.

In the end, nobody knows what will happen in the future. However, if you ask plenty of questions and strive to learn as much as you can about the world of finance and investment, remain open-minded and acknowledge when you might need to alter or rethink your perspective, *and* maintain a long-term focus and consistent approach, you'll find that your odds of investment success are as good as anyone's.

⋗◆⋖

# CHAPTER 19

# Yield and Returns

We've discussed various things you'll need to know about investing. But two areas we haven't covered are historical returns and yield. Use this data to choose a fund or funds. This takes emotion out of the formula. For this reason, it is a good idea to have some sense of how the 10 sector specific mutual funds or ETFs you'll be watching, studying and investing in have fared over various periods of time. If one has performed extremely well for five years, for instance, while another has done very poorly, then it might be worth betting on--or should we say investing in--a reversal of fortunes.

Recent chart displaying vanguard's ETF sector funds yield:

| Fund Name | YTD Yield | 1 Year | 5 Year | 10 Year | Since Inception |
|-----------|-----------|--------|--------|---------|-----------------|
| *Consumer Discretionary | 10.47% | 16.72% | 19.18% | 10.96% | 9.45% |
| Consumer Staples | 3.32% | 9.49% | 15.12% | 11.24% | 10.50% |
| Energy | - 11.39% | - 21.66% | 3.09% | 4.71% | 7.72% |
| Financials | 2.55% | 3.69% | 12.42% | 1.24% | 1.90% |
| *Health Care | 6.51% | 7.88% | 20.63% | 11.39% | 9.90% |

| Industrials | - 0.51% | 1.02% | 13.67% | 8.43% | 8.67% |
| :---: | :---: | :---: | :---: | :---: | :---: |
| *Information Technology | 8.94% | 10.54% | 14.59% | 9.94% | 7.65% |
| Materials | - 6.53% | - 5.81% | 7.89% | 8.14% | 8.11% |
| REIT | - 0.94% | 5.91% | 12.08% | 7.88% | 9.31% |
| Telecommunication Services | 3.81% | 1.57% | 10.25% | 7.98% | 9.32% |
| Utilities | - 8.19% | - 0.74% | 11.11% | 7.53% | 9.32% |

* Indicates funds with good yield currently - Indicates poor yield currently
All these funds except Financials have performed well since inception.

By looking at the YTD Yield, it is easy to identify a fund that has current yields that will grow your investment. When you buy that fund whose yield is good it is likely to continue its growth until it falls. By scanning the history of yield it becomes obvious that these 10 ETFs vary over time. This simply means that after you purchase any fund it is wise to monitor that fund.

Purchasing the best yield and watching your investment is an easy method of getting started. You'll learn as you observe your selected fund over time. If you are interested in more, then you can drill down deeper into the funds and their prospectuses.

Measuring performance of funds is yield. While it can have a variety of meanings--some might use it to describe the gains you realize from investing in an asset that has gone up in price--the term generally refers to the cash you receive from a particular investment. If you purchased 10,000 USD of the Consumer Discretionary fund, it would have amassed a 10.57% in growth. Yield is like the interest paid on a savings account. If you deposit money into a savings account your "yield" is the value of the interest you receive dividend by the amount of money you started with.

# All 10 of These ETF Funds also
# pay a Dividend Quarterly

A dividend means money is paid back to you on top of the gains in the price of the fund. Dividends are paid back by reinvesting in more shares or money. The investor decides how the dividends are to be paid back when you buy the fund. So your yield reflects the cash paid out to shareholders as dividends, relative to the amount of your stake. In other words, it's not just what happens to prices that matters. How much cash you receive for owning something is an equally important consideration. Dividends are a bonus payment the investor receives for simply holding that fund in their account!

In reality, it is the combination of price changes and cash payouts, the total return that matters most. If the price of a fund goes up 5% and your investment account is also credited with the equivalent of 3% worth of dividends (paid out by the companies in the fund's underlying portfolio) over the course of 12 months, then you've made a total return of 8% during that period. Not too shabby.

As with other data about economics, business conditions and individual companies, information about sector specific mutual funds and exchange-traded funds past performance and yields is readily available, either through your broker, the fund sponsors, the media or the Internet. Make sure that data becomes a key part of your wealth-building arsenal. Having chosen a sector fund you like, it is time to buy and begin compounding money!

# CHAPTER 20

# Putting Your Money to Work

At this point, you'll probably be itching to take the plunge. But first, take a deep breath. Yes, sometimes opportunity knocks for just a second, but when it comes to investing, it generally makes sense to move forward at a measured pace. In other words, opportunity is *always* knocking. Walk through the steps you took up until now and see if anything might have been missed or mishandled. Is your account set up? Did you make your initial deposit?

Then you'll need to think about the process itself. Have you taken time to learn about the options that you should be focusing on? Do you understand the ins and outs of the various sector-related investments, including why some might do well or poorly when others don't? Have you thought about your own knowledge, experience and skills to see where you might have the best odds of choosing wisely? Regardless of where your expertise lies, you should let it help you make what will prove to be an important decision.

Assuming you've done all that and feel ready to act, it still might make sense to stand back and keep an eye on those investments for a while before pulling the trigger. As with many things in life, people occasionally have second thoughts about the decisions they make after chewing them over. Remember to sleep on your decision and let cybernetics work. People often sleep on something and wake up more convinced than ever that they made the right call. Your subconscious mind is always working, even while you are asleep--why not take advantage of that?

# Pulling the Trigger

OK, so you're ready to begin. What happens next? The actual mechanics of trading will vary depending on the firm you have partnered with and the security you'll be investing in. If it's a mutual fund, you typically will only be able to add or take out funds once a day, generally before a preset cut-off time. In these cases, the transactions are typically referred to as exchanges, rather than as buys or sells, because you will invariably be moving money from one fund, which might be a money market fund, to another. The prices you transact at will be the closing values on that day.

Things work a little differently when you are investing in exchange-traded funds. In this case, you will be asking the representative, or using the telephone or online trading tools your firm provides, to either buy or sell some quantity of ETF shares that is equivalent to the amount of money you wish to invest. If it is a purchase, the amount you owe will either be deducted from the cash in your account, or the balance invested in a money market fund, on the settlement date (which is typically three days after you transact). Typically, the trade is done during market hours fixed by exchanges.

Regardless of which kind of fund you invest in or trading approach you take, your financial intermediary will report back to you in one way or another to let you know what was done. Most firms are required to mail you a written confirmation unless you opt for emails or other methods. But those are usually sent out one day or even days after the fact. Before then, you can usually find out what did or did not transpire from the representative by telephone or via the online trading software the firm may have available.

At that point, you will have skin in the game.

⇒◆⇐

# CHAPTER 21

# Keeping Tabs on Your Future

Putting your money to work is the beginning. You are now an investor and will need to keep a careful eye on your investments--most likely, nobody else will--and ensure that things remain on course. Virtually every trading day, and perhaps every minute of every day that markets are open, prices will fluctuate, and so, too, will the value of your holdings. Some of you will have the urge to sign in to an online account every other minute to see what is happening; others might be happy enough to wait until they receive their monthly or quarterly statements.

As always, it is best to strike some sort of balance. If you are overly eager, you may find that your investing zeal starts interfering with other areas of your life. On the other hand, if you don't pay enough attention to what is happening, you could discover that things have changed for the worst, without you even realizing it, making it difficult for you to make the necessary adjustments or rethink your perspectives.

One of three things will happen: the prices will remain the same, move up or go down. You should also be aware that it will be hard to avoid feeling great when things are going well and your investments are increasing in value; conversely, it will be difficult to avoid being upset when they head the other way. Fear is often experienced when your balance goes down and greed kicks in when your balance go up. These are perfectly normal reactions which even the most knowledgeable and experienced investors work hard to overcome. It is generally not a good idea to be emotional when it comes to matters of money. Don't make snap judgements on how your emotions are being triggered.

Professional money managers rely on a variety of strategies to try to minimize the effects that our biases and emotions can have on decisions and actions. Some like to keep a log or mental notes, updated regularly, with such details as:

1. Why they made the decision they did and what influenced their timing.
2. What they expected to see in future.
3. Whether their expectations were on the mark.
4. How they would know if their decisions were correct.
5. What they would do if they began losing a lot of money or if they suddenly realized they were wrong or want to get out of a buy.

They might also review their holdings and strategy on a regular basis to see if the reasons they made one investment over another still make sense. They make it a point to stay informed about what is going on at the companies and in the industries they are focused on, and they purposely seek out both sides of the story to lessen the risk, otherwise they will only see what they want to see. It is all too easy to think that any decision we make will be correct and won't ever change, but as we all know, the only constant in our lives is that things change.

Seasoned investors also work hard to stay on top of other developments that could affect their investments, including paying attention to trends in the broad market. Most watch CNN.

As long as you don't get overly caught up in the excitement of it all, staying in touch with what is happening to your investments will help you in any number of ways. When you pay attention to something, you naturally see more than you would if you didn't. You begin to understand what issues and which news matters, as well as what doesn't. You'll be learning by doing and observing. Over time, your interest should inspire you to want to know more about what is happening and why, eventually enabling you to make better, more informed decisions. You can always balance and fine-tune your investments.

# CHAPTER 22

# When Things Go Wrong

It's been said before, but it bears repeating: *"Nobody knows what will happen in the future."* Whether someone is smart, well-informed, experienced or lucky; the odds that he will be able to accurately predict tomorrow's news more than once or twice are somewhere between zero and none. However, just because we don't know what any particular day will bring doesn't mean we can't narrow down the range of possibilities. Can we know if a healthy 50-year old person will die tomorrow of natural causes? No. But can we say that he will pass away sometime during the next 50 years? Absolutely.

The same holds true for markets. Can we know whether a market or our funds will, over the course of time, rise or fall? Individual companies can fail, but using diversified mutual funds ends the risk of a big crash, sending your balance to zero. Nonetheless, by watching, we will know. It's possible that at some point in the future the stock market, as well as all your fund investments, could crash.

Now, what do we mean by "crash?" Well, that sort of depends on your perspective, but most experts would probably define it as a decline of 20% or more over some relatively short period. Is it possible that something much worse could happen--such as the value of the world indexes being totally wiped out? Again, it's possible, but the odds of this are virtually nil. If this worst case scenario happened, then life itself as the civilization we know would probably be over. Given the connection between Main Street and Wall Street to the rest of the world's survival, you shouldn't worry.

Happily, the prospect of a wipeout, especially when you are invested in a fund that holds a diversified group of companies, is not something to be overly concerned about. But if and when prices fall and the value of your investments declines, it's important to understand how that might affect you and what you might need to do about it. As suggested earlier, big swings in your portfolio can trigger similar swings in your state of mind. While any one individual might not react in the same way, we tend to experience one of two emotions when it comes to matters of money: greed and fear.

When the value of our investments increases, especially if it happens quickly, it can make us feel powerful and secure, and our self-confidence can rise very fast. Unfortunately, such feelings can feed an intense, selfish and impulsive desire to have more of the same, which can lead us to abandon a conservative strategy in favor of making a quick buck or acting without really thinking things through. When greed takes over, investors often find themselves chasing today's winners and betting that those investments that have risen quickly recently will keep doing so in future.

When our investments lose value, it can trigger a different reaction. We may feel panic and despair, as if it is only a matter of time before we're headed into poverty and desperation. Some of us may feel like a deer frozen in the headlights, unable to make any decisions that might be necessary. Alternatively, we may panic and try to dash for the exits. Although it made sense for our ancestors from long ago to react without thinking when they faced potentially dangerous uncertainty, such a perspective is not much help when it comes to investing.

There have been various occasions when investors let their immediate fears cause them to throw out the baby with the bathwater. During the Great Depression of the 1930s, many people were gripped by fear, and it led any number of them to do things they later regretted or which caused them and their loved ones a lot of pain. Certainly, many were terrified by the relentless selling they were seeing in financial markets, but in going with the crowd, they missed an opportunity to secure their future that would not come around again for several decades.

# Stop Loss Strategy

The fact is, the time to exit an investment is not when you are fearful or emotional. The time to get out is when things happen that you have decided on *before* making the investment. Known as a "stop loss" strategy, such a plan of action is designed to ensure that you are in charge of your investments, and not the other way around. Although there are a number of approaches you might take, the most common are those that are based on some combination of price and time.

A price-based stop loss is relatively easy to grasp. You determine in advance how much of your initial investment that you are willing to lose-- say, perhaps 10%--and if the value of your holdings falls to that point, you arrange to sell or exchange it for something else, typically a money market fund or cash, on the next day. By doing that, you are acknowledging that it was a mistake and you are clearing the decks for something better. That doesn't mean you won't feel bad about having lost the money--anybody would. What it does mean, though, is that you will be thinking like a long-term investor who understands that sometimes things go wrong. Remember, even the best major league batters only score a hit one time out of three!

There is always the possibility that you will be getting out of an investment at the wrong time. But that doesn't matter. The key to wealth building is to work with a consistent long-term approach. Like great football coaches have often said, *"It is not the occasional brilliant maneuvers that win ball games; every first down keeps the ball in play and that leads to long-term success."*

———◇———

# CHAPTER 23

# Don't Forget the Taxman

[Taxes are for those who invest in American markets. All other
investors in other countries can bypass this chapter.]

It's been said, "*There are only two things that are certain in this world:
death and taxes.*" The former is something most people probably don't spend
a lot of time thinking about, figuring it is mostly out of their hands. But
when it comes to what you might have to hand over to the government, you
do have some measure of control.

For Americans, when managing your day-to-day affairs, you can try to
adjust when you make certain tax-deductible payments or receive taxable
income, so that the net result works out in your favor. If, for example, you
have had a great year financially and you find that your tax rate will be
higher than you initially anticipated, you might want to consider prepaying
expenses that aren't technically due until next year, thereby reducing this
year's taxable income. Alternatively, if you will be getting a year-end bonus
or are an entrepreneur who is expecting a large payment, you might ask that
the checks be delayed until January.

When it comes to your investments, how you go about optimizing
your tax position depends to a large extent on what sort of account your
investments are held in. As mentioned earlier, one way to invest is through
a tax-deferred account. IRAs and 401(k)s not only let you invest a portion
of your income tax-free, they also allow you to avoid paying taxes on
whatever dividends, interest or profits you realize on that investment until

you start withdrawing the proceeds. Before that, your money compounds tax-free. However, there are rules about how much you can invest each year with such plans and when you can or must make withdrawals. You may have to pay penalties if you need the money sooner than the rules generally allow. For many MGTOW, choosing to use some of your assets to enjoy life makes the penalty easy to pay.

In contrast, if your investments are held in a taxable account, there are a variety of decisions you can make that could benefit you at the taxman's expense. The first is probably the easiest: when prices move in your favor, don't sell or switch out of your winners until you need or want to. In most cases, you don't owe any taxes on investment gains until you decide to cash out. In addition, if you hold onto an investment for an extended period of time, generally 12 months or more (though the laws are subject to change), whatever you realize on the sale will be taxed at a lower than the normal rate, known as the long-term capital gains rate.

Taxes shouldn't be your only guiding principle, of course. While many people do whatever they can to avoid paying the government a penny, investment decisions should always take precedence. If, as discussed earlier, your stop loss strategy leaves you with no choice but to sell your fund, then you must do so, regardless of the tax consequences. And while it might seem like a good idea to hold off on realizing a big gain, if the circumstances have changed and there is a risk, your investment could decline sharply as a result, then the tax considerations should definitely come secondary.

It's worth bearing in mind that even those who consider themselves experienced and well informed have a hard time understanding and keeping up with the thousands of lines of text and the millions of words that comprise the various federal, state and local tax codes. If there's any doubt about what you can or cannot do, or what the tax or other financial consequences of any decision might be, you should check with an expert.

Some readers may know the author spent decades working in professional roller derby. The next and final chapter was inspired by two young male skaters of today's leagues who share a common problem and represent millions of other men.

————⟫◆⟪————

# CHAPTER 24

# Nickolas Gets Lucky

The bedroom is bathed in darkness. Two entwined bodies are pumping, and animal heat and the unmistakable scent of pussy and musk fill the air. A solitary bead of sweat runs down Nick's forehead and drips onto the face of Michelle, who is gyrating beneath him.

Her breath catches and she gasps. "Please, Nick! You're hurting me—" She groans and tries to wriggle away.

"Hold still, bitch. I know you like that." Nick's voice is quiet and commanding, and he lets out a chuckle. There is no doubt as to whom is dominant here. Nick is in control. Michelle thrashes from side to side, trying to get away. Tears run down her delicate chin.

"You're too big, Nick. I can't—" She gasps again.

Nick's eyes narrow. "What's the matter, slut? Can't you handle it?"

She pushes him away and crosses her arms over her breasts. Nick grabs her wrists and pins them to the pillow. "Shut up! You're my slave tonight."

"Please, Nick. Take me!" Michelle's eyes glisten with a mixture of excitement and fear.

Nick presses his mouth against hers. He forces her legs apart and jackhammers his cock into her pussy.

*Brrring!* His eyes snapped open. He rolled to the edge of the bed and flicked off the alarm. "That damn dream again." The vision melted away. He waited for his morning erection to go down. When it didn't, he jacked off quickly, reaching climax as he pictured Michelle's tear-stained face. He wiped his hand on the sheet and reached for his phone so he could check his e-mails.

When twenty-five-year-old Nickolas Stern first opened Michelle Carson's profile on OKCupid, he couldn't believe that this stunning blonde, with icy green eyes and high cheekbones, was single. Nick hadn't had sex for months. In desperation, he had turned to the Internet. As he flicked through her photos, he felt his cock engorging with blood. He leaned closer to the screen.

24, 5'7", SLIM. I'M TRUSTING, AFFECTIONATE, AND LOYAL. I LISTEN TO ALL KINDS OF MUSIC, ESPECIALLY JAZZ, POP, AND CLASSICAL. A BIT OF A HOMEBODY. LOVE TO CURL UP WITH A STEAMING MUG OF COCOA AND A GOOD CHICK FLICK! MY FAVORITE NOVEL IS THE NOTEBOOK BY NICKOLAS SPARKS.

It sounded promising. Nick opened his own profile. Compared to Michelle's, his self-description cut straight to the chase.

25, 6'2", ATHLETIC. I'M A TECH HEAD SYSTEMS ENGINEER LOOKING FOR ROMANCE. GET READY TO BE TREATED BETTER THAN ANY GUY HAS EVER TREATED YOU. BONUS POINTS IF YOU LIKE MAJOR LEAGUE BASEBALL.

Nick decided to write her a message. Being new to the world of Internet dating, he struggled to find the right words. He rewrote the text six times before hitting Send. Then, in a moment of excruciating self-doubt, he reread what he had written.

WELCOME TO PHILADELPHIA! THIS IS MY HOMETOWN, SO I'D LOVE TO SHOW YOU AROUND. WE COULD VISIT THE NATIONAL PARK, LIBERTY BELL, AND THE EVER-POPULAR STATUE OF ROCKY BALBOA LOL. Upbeat, casual. And he'd managed to project a chivalrous air, rather than that of a sex-starved hound. Women generally don't appreciate guys who want to immediately jump on them. The trick was to come across as an ally without getting sequestered in the friend zone. Nick's body felt feverish and his palms were moist as he compulsively checked his phone, awaiting her reply. He knew it was too soon, so he put his computer to sleep and tried to busy himself with other stuff. But his balls kept tingling, and he checked his inbox every ten minutes over the course of the day. He couldn't stop thinking how much he wanted to be close to Michelle. He wondered how her skin would feel, and how her kiss might taste. When he opened his inbox for what seemed like the thousandth time, he saw that she had left him a message.

HEY NICK! HOW ARE YOU DOING? THANKS FOR YOUR KIND OFFER. I'D LOVE FOR YOU TO SHOW ME AROUND SOMETIME. LET ME KNOW WHEN YOU'RE FREE!

Wow. Nick's heart began to race. As he texted back, he had to remind himself to keep things light and friendly. GREAT TO HEAR FROM YOU. SO WHAT BRINGS YOU TO PHILLY

IT WAS TIME TO GET OUT OF PITTSBURGH. I LIKED IT, BUT I JUST COULDN'T FIND WORK OUT THERE

WHAT DO YOU DO

I'M THE CUSTOMER COORDINATOR AT A PUBLISHING COMPANY

*Yes! A connection.* He took a deep breath. SOUNDS COOL, DO YOU LIKE IT

IT'S OKAY I GUESS

Their dialogue continued for about an hour. Finally, Michelle began to wind things up. I SHOULD PROBABLY GET BACK TO WORK

Nick felt his heart sink. Not wishing to appear weak, he tried to sound as casual as possible. YEAH I HAVE TO RUN. GREAT TALKING TO YOU

BYE … FOR NOW.

A huge grin spread across Nick's face. TALK SOON

When he pressed Send, Nick imagined an electronic kiss whizzing through fiber-optic cables. It had gone so well! He was pumped. There was a dull throbbing sensation in his groin. He looked down. His cock was hard as iron.

During the daytime, Michelle was elusive. Nick was usually the one to initiate conversation, and it would take her a while to respond, always keeping it brief. Most of their chats took place in the evenings; that was when Michelle seemed to come alive. Despite his growing affection for her, Nick kept the tone light. He never discussed religion or politics. One night, Michelle messaged him shortly after eleven o'clock. Nick was surprised. For her, this was uncharacteristically late.

HEY. WHAT YOU UP TO?

Nick's curiosity was piqued. IN BED. YOU?

ME TOO. ARE YOU ALONE?

His heart began to pound as he pictured her lying in her bed. Was she naked? OF COURSE. WHO ELSE WOULD BE HERE?

YOU SAID IN YOUR PROFILE YOU'RE LOOKING FOR ROMANCE. MAYBE YOU ALREADY FOUND IT?

Nick's mouth felt dry. What was her deal? He reminded himself to keep his tone light. NOPE. STILL SEARCHING HA

IT'S PRETTY LATE. WHY AREN'T YOU ASLEEP?

WHY AREN'T YOU? ;)

SAME REASON AS YOU, PROBABLY

Nick couldn't quite decide whether her banter was annoying or sexy. Was she getting on his case or angling for phone sex? He felt like she was testing him somehow. He didn't want to come across as horny. On the other hand, he didn't want to appear disinterested. I CAN THINK OF A FEW WAYS TO PASS THE TIME

SUCH AS?

By this time, Nick was already hard. Should he invite her over, or would that seem too forward? READING A BOOK OR WATCHING TV MAYBE? Damn. Had he just blown his chance to get laid tonight?

I SHOULD TRY TO SLEEP

NICE CHATTING WITH YOU. SLEEP WELL

YOU TOO

He jacked off, envisioning his cum splashing her face. The following day, he reread their conversation, wondering whether his responses should have been a little more suggestive. Within a few days of that late-night chat, they began to speak on the phone. Michelle's sweet, girly voice made him feel strong and masculine. They flirted a lot, but never directly addressed the topic of sex. He could sometimes hear the smile in Michelle's voice as she toyed and teased with him, bringing him gradually closer to the breaking point.

"I wonder whether it's time to start thinking about taking the first step of our journey together," Nick said. "Do you know what I'm talking about?"

"Everyone needs sex," Michelle said casually, laughing.

That was almost too easy. Nick's stomach flipped. "I have some experience in that department."

"So have I. Not all of it was positive."

"Really? What do you mean?"

"I've been hurt. My heart's been broken before."

Picturing the worst, Nick was overwhelmed by a wave of empathy. He tried to clear the lump in his throat. "I'm really sorry to hear that."

"It's okay, but it's made it difficult for me to trust men." Her voice sounded thin and hollow.

Nick wondered what he could say to reassure her that he was different and would supersede her expectations.

"Relationships can be so painful," mused Michelle.

Nick pictured her perched on the edge of her bed, fighting tears.

"I mean, you can totally fall for someone, and then you find out it isn't a good fit. Because he is just too different and too far away."

"I know what you mean," Nick said in a soothing voice.

"You do?"

"Sure. But not all men are the same. And you have to learn how to love again. If you can't trust anyone, you'll end up alone."

"True, but at least I wouldn't get hurt."

"If you take a risk, you may lose, but if you never risk anything, you've already lost out."

"Wow, that's deep. Especially considering you're a techie."

"Thanks. Not all tech guys are boring." Nick was glad that his wild stab at explaining his philosophical take on life and love had washed with her. He could feel her mood lifting.

"I love movies, don't you?" Michelle said, apropos of nothing. "Have you seen *Fifty Shades of Grey*?"

Nick laughed. "Who hasn't?"

"I liked that. I liked it a lot," she said quietly and evenly.

Nick felt she was sending him a signal, loud and clear. He swallowed the lump in his throat. "I see. So you like it rough?" He awaited her response with bated breath.

"Let's just say I like a man to take the lead in bed." Her voice had a playful ring to it. "I respond to male dominance. Nothing too heavy! A little spanking can be fun."

Nick coughed loudly, trying to ignore his growing erection. "I can be quite forceful," Nick said. He was turned on by rough sex fantasies, but he had never experimented with role-play or any other forms of BDSM.

"Tell me more about your fantasies," Nick commanded.

Michelle yawned. "Maybe some other time. I should try to get some sleep."

"Oh, okay. Sure." Nick's boner died on the spot. How did he keep messing this up? Or was she always running hot and cold? Later that night, he masturbated while imagining her wrists manacled to the bedposts.

The next few evenings, they talked on the phone. Their conversations ran late into the night, and Michelle would sometimes even doze off. Nick talked about his job, and Michelle seemed to be impressed by the fact that he worked hard, so he began to exaggerate the importance of his job. He told her he was planning to buy a motorbike. This wasn't true, but she reacted so enthusiastically that he began to research motorbikes and often filled her in on which bike he was considering purchasing.

"Do you like sports?"

"Of course. I'm a guy, aren't I? My favorite is baseball."

"As in, you play? Or do you just sit on the couch and watch?"

Nick wasn't the best sportsman, but he certainly wasn't a couch potato. He went to the gym twice a week. On Sundays, he sometimes went for a quick jog through his neighborhood.

"I like to play, but it's hard to find the time because my career is so demanding," he said.

"Sure," said Michelle soothingly. "You have so much responsibility, so many people working under you. But more responsibility means more money, right?"

"Yeah, but it also means more stress. Money's important, but it's not the be-all and end-all."

"It's important. You must want to get married and have a family. Kids are expensive."

Nick had never given it much thought. As far as he was concerned, he still had plenty of time. At around thirty, he would start to consider it, he decided. That was a good age to have children. He knew that this line of conversation would get her panties moist, so he didn't immediately change the topic.

"Of course. I definitely want to have children. By the time that happens, I plan on having some serious money in the bank."

"You're a smart guy. And you're six-foot-one, huh? You seem perfect. Do you have a six-pack?"

Nick was glad she had changed the subject. "You'll find out soon enough." He was a handsome man and had always been aware of it.

"You're funny. I like that in a guy," she sighed. "Have you ever served in the military?"

Why had she asked him that? Maybe she had a fetish for guys in uniform. Nick had never been in the military, though he had seriously considered it after graduating from high school, but in the end he had gone straight to university.

"I've thought about it, but I never signed up," he told Michelle. "I'm good with guns."

"Hmm," she said suggestively.

He laughed. "My uncle has a shooting range and I used to go there sometimes to let off steam. But if I'm honest, I prefer computers."

"I see." Michelle paused. Nick could hear her breathing into the receiver.

"How about we go out for dinner sometime?" Nick felt his face flush. The question had come out of nowhere.

They went on a dinner date the following night, followed by another and yet another. Nick picked up the tab every time, but he didn't mind. Michelle was a great girl and everything was going perfectly. As he came to know her better, there was plenty about her that interested him beyond sex, but by date number five, he thought it was about time that she put out. He booked a table for two at Vetri, the most exclusive restaurant in Philly. The cheapest item on the menu was a hundred and fifty bucks. He knew how much money impressed her. That pussy would soon be his for the taking.

---

**N**ick stopped the car. "Here we are, Mademoiselle!"

He climbed out and walked around to open Michelle's door. He offered his arm and she gracefully laced her arm through his. They approached the entrance of the restaurant; Nick held the door open for a couple whose freckled, red-haired son trailed behind them. Nick gave the boy a wink and a grin. "Good evening, young man," Nick said, bowing. The boy giggled and beamed at Nick before running off to catch up with his parents.

"Oh my God. You'd make such a great father," Michelle said with a dreamy look in her eyes. She gave him a sultry smile, pursing her luscious lips.

*Me? A father? A role model?* Nick's heart swelled with manly pride as he looked at Michelle, whose eyes were glistening. He liked the idea of passing on his traits and talents and knowledge to a son. "I guess that might be true," Nick said humbly, but he glided into the restaurant with his head held high and his shoulders thrown back.

Once they had been seated at their table, Michelle smiled prettily. "What a wonderful place. And you got us the best table! You must be so well-connected." She played with an earring.

Nick shrugged, feigning modesty. "I know some people," he said enigmatically. The truth was, he had stopped by earlier that afternoon and had slipped the maître d' two hundred bucks for the table and another hundred to address him by name. He was happy she liked his choice for the evening. He felt like a real man.

"I could get used to this kind of treatment," Michelle said coyly, insinuating that he had better keep it up, but also that she could imagine them being together for a while.

Nick's heart swelled. Michelle ordered the saffron fusilli with lobster and Pernod. Nick ordered pistachio fettuccine with artichokes. Michelle looked gorgeous, and he wondered if they would have sex that night. He had been way too polite for far too long.

He cleared his throat. "Remember when we first chatted? I couldn't believe how sexy you sounded."

"That's such a sweet thing to say," Michelle said, smiling shyly. The sommelier approached their table. Michelle ordered Bonarda without even glancing at the wine card.

"You know your wines," he said.

Michelle grinned.

"Are you trying to get me drunk?" he said. "Maybe I'm not that kind of guy."

"Oh, Nicky!" She laughed giddily.

When the food arrived, Michelle unfurled her napkin and tucked it into her dress. Nick inhaled the earthy odor of pistachio. They tucked in eagerly. For a while, they ate in silence.

"So have I succeeded in sweeping you off your feet with my charm and stunning good looks?" Nick asked, with a glint of humor in his eyes.

Michelle gave him a seductive smirk. "Who said you were handsome? Your mom?"

"She's a wise woman."

Michelle laughed out loud before dabbing her lips with the napkin. She was glowing with excitement. Nick signaled to the waiter to top up Michelle's glass.

"Maybe you're the one who's trying to get me drunk tonight," Michelle said.

"Just taking care of my lady. Is that so wrong?" Nick gazed tenderly into her eyes. He wondered what she looked like when she orgasmed.

"Such a gentleman." She drained her glass and set it down. "How was your week? Did you have that big meeting at work?"

She looked so pretty and she smelled incredible. Nick felt a little dizzy. "Yeah. It was about data security. You know, how to keep information secure."

"Well, after Ashley Madison was hacked—"

Nick gulped. "Yes, well."

"Can you imagine over thirty million people could be married and still be on the prowl for sex? No one takes their vows seriously."

He wondered if those people were as in love as he was. He couldn't say the word love to her yet. "Maybe they fell out of love?"

"That's silly." She scrunched up her face in a cute way, shaking her head.

"If you really love someone, it should last forever." If he could only gain her trust, maybe she would tie him up and lick his balls.

"Oh, I don't know. I'd like to believe that, but you know, a lifetime is quite a long time."

Nick blinked. "What are you saying?"

Michelle peered down into her wine glass. "People change over time. It's easy to be faithful at the beginning of a relationship, but how about in the long run?"

Nick's stomach lurched. "I take your point," he said quietly.

Michelle's bearing had turned melancholy, and Nick felt as though the opportunity was slipping away. "Not all men are the same. You really have to believe that."

Michelle smiled and nodded her head. The two of them shared a contemplative silence.

"I'm thinking of buying this eighty-inch Ultra-HD TV," Nick said brightly, in an effort to lighten the mood.

"Sounds nice!"

"Yeah, I like to watch sports. And the picture quality on those things is fantastic."

Michelle nodded. "You said you enjoy new technology."

"Yeah, and there's some really awesome stuff out there. I just looked at some of these 4K TVs. They're a bit expensive, but the quality is amazing and 4K content is becoming widely available on the Internet. Even on Netflix or YouTube."

Michelle gulped her wine and gazed at him with shiny eyes.

Nick rambled on, wondering how to come back to the subject of sex. "Sure, and I'm looking at a new high-speed desktop to have at home. I mean I have a laptop, of course, but in terms of processor speed and everything, desktops are some next-level shit."

"Seems like you're buying an awful lot of stuff. Are you sure you're making enough money?" The question hung in the air.

"I'm starting at IBM on sixty-five grand a year," he said candidly. "I'm in data warehousing and plan to move into application security systems." He forked salad into his mouth while staring Michelle straight in the eyes.

Michelle looked suitably impressed. "That sounds wonderful."

Beneath the table, Nick's balls tightened. He leaned across the table, and Michelle closed her eyes.

"More wine?" the waiter said cheerily. He seemed unaware that he had just interrupted what was supposed to be a passionate kiss.

Nick rolled his eyes. Michelle giggled and blushed. The waiter filled the glasses and walked away. Nick felt a warm hand on his thigh. The sensation sent bolts of sensual energy tingling up and down his spine.

"I think I'm falling for you," Michelle said.

Nick leaned across the table and locked her in a passionate kiss. When they broke off for air, Michelle composed herself. "This is one of the best restaurants in town! Behave yourself." She winked and squeezed his thigh under the table.

"How do you expect me to behave myself when I'm looking at such a beautiful woman?"

"You think I'm beautiful?"

"Well, from what I can see. But I haven't seen it all yet."

Michelle gave him a knowing smile. They gazed into each other's eyes. Nick said, "It's our fifth date already—" His words dangled in the air.

"*And?*"

"Nothing! Just an observation. It's going well so far, don't you think?"

Michelle smiled. "So you can count to five. So can I. And I have a five-date rule." She leaned across the table. With her mouth close to his ear, she whispered, "I always wait until the fifth date before having sex."

Nick's heart began to race. "Does that mean I'll get lucky tonight?"

"Who knows? I'd say you'll get lucky tonight if you make me lucky."

"What does that mean?"

Michelle grinned. "How about we go to your place tonight?"

———

**T**he light in the bedroom glowed softly against the sheets while Nick explored Michelle with his fingers. The soft curves of her naked body thrilled him to the bone. He ran his hands over her flat belly, her supple breasts, and around her back to grip her tight buttocks. Michelle moaned softly in the darkness, her breath coming in short whimpers. Everything about her was perfect, the way she looked, felt, tasted and smelled.

Michelle massaged Nick's biceps and eased them slowly to his shoulders and back. His body quivered beneath her touch. She turned him over onto his back and ran her tongue down his chest and stomach to his groin. She took his cock deep into her mouth. Nick's breathing grew faster as she savored him like a lollipop. He pushed her off and flung her onto the bed. Mounting her, he spread her legs and drove his cock roughly into her. She was so wet that he slid right in.

"Yesss," she moaned.

Nick's hands explored her body as his cock explored her cunt. With each thrust of his hips, he went closer, deeper.

"God, you're so tight," he moaned.

The pleasure mounted until it seemed almost unbearable. Nick exploded inside her and she climaxed immediately afterwards. He was amazed at how he could feel every little pulse and twitch. Afterwards, they lay gasping for air. Nick's heart was pounding, and his chest heaved as they relaxed in each other's arms.

Michelle made a contented purring sound. She was like a kitten with a bowl of cream.

"That was so good." Nick sighed.

Michelle sat up with a start. "What time is it?" she said, seeming agitated.

"About ten. Why?" He couldn't figure out what had caused her mood to suddenly change.

Michelle stretched and got up. "I had better get home."

"You're very welcome to spend the night."

"I should go."

"Are you okay? Did I do something wrong?" Nick sensed that a trapdoor was about to fall open beneath him and send him tumbling into an abyss.

"No, not at all." Michelle found her panties and started putting them on. "It's just—well, I need to tell you something."

"What?" Nick laughed in an effort to disguise his panic. "Are we on Jerry Springer? You're going to tell me you were actually born a man!"

"I have to get home to my kids."

Nick's gut sank. His mind seemed to dissolve. "Kids?"

"Um, yeah. I have three." Michelle zipped her dress and smiled innocently at him.

Nick was speechless. He clutched the bedsheet.

"Is there a problem?" she asked, sounding almost aggressive.

Nick's heart thudded in his chest as he tried to process the information. "You never mentioned them. How long have we been talking?"

"We all have our secrets and surprises," Michelle said coyly. "For example, you never told me how, um—*gifted* you are."

Nick felt his cheeks flush with pride. A smile crept across his lips. Despite the rush he got from the ego boost, Nick felt queasy and his head was spinning. He ran his fingers through his hair as dark clouds gathered in his mind. Michelle was standing in the doorway, applying lipstick. She blew a kiss over her shoulder and sashayed out.

Nick exhaled and sank back onto the pillow. As he stared up at the ceiling, his thoughts whirled like a small tornado. What the hell was that? He tapped a finger against his chest in time to the seconds ticking on the wall clock. "I'm dating a woman with children," he said, to see how it sounded. He reached for his phone and Googled *dating single mothers.*

The top result was a YouTube video by a guy named Tom Leykis who said you should never marry a single mother. A man phoned in to the talk show and shared his experience of dating a woman whose children had been fathered by her previous boyfriend. It was almost as if he was describing Nick's relationship with Michelle. Memories from the past few months flooded his mind. Little things Michelle had said, small hints and gestures, all slowly fell into place. It was a puzzle with many moving parts. When the video ended, Nick immediately watched it again.

Over the next few days, the uneasy feeling kept growing inside him. Nick began to re-examine his relationship with Michelle. He still felt a deep attraction to this beautiful, sexy young woman. She was great in bed and he longed to feel her legs wrapped around his waist again. But he hadn't liked the way she'd withheld the fact that she had children, and then oh-so-casually mentioned it right after the first time they had sex. It seemed callous at best, and manipulative at worst. And then she'd flattered him with the comment about the size of his cock. Nick rolled his eyes. How could he have been so blind?

Nick began to research the topic in earnest so as to arm himself with information.

It wasn't long before he stumbled across a movement called Men Going Their Own Way (MGTOW), whose website contained a wealth of information that seemed to be of profound significance for all men. How had he never heard of this before? Where else could men find out about potentially toxic heterosexual relationships? The ideas it presented seemed obvious, but at its heart, the matter was an incredibly complex one. Nick longed to know more.

A YouTube search led to another revelatory video: Stefan Molyneux's *The Dangers of Dating a Single Mom.* Molyneux really knew his stuff, and he laid things out with alarming clarity. Nick found a great number of videos in which men recounted their negative experiences with women. Nick felt that he had found his mentors, and he wondered how he had survived for so long without them. He decided he would confront Michelle and try to initiate an open, honest discussion. That night, Nick hardly slept. His dreams swirled with these newly discovered ideas and information.

———

The summer air, alive with the smell of lilac and avocado, lifted Nick's spirits. The perfumed haze rose above the grandeur of the library. Nick could almost hear the clicking of puzzle pieces falling into place inside his mind. After a week spent deep in thought, he found the solution which glimmered like the sun in the sky. He finally had the answers to all of his questions. Nick knew he had finally found his truth.

"Mmm. Freshly cut grass and the scent of late morning mist," Nick sighed.

"I'm hungry!" Michelle giggled, batting her eyelashes.

They strolled along the sidewalk. "I have fried chicken, potato salad and a chilled Pinot Grigio," he said.

Michelle tucked her arm through the crook of his elbow and leaned her head against his shoulder. "Did you make it yourself?"

"Of course." He guided her towards a picnic table.

"This is sweet," Michelle said as she sat down.

"I enjoyed preparing it." Nick spread out a plastic tablecloth and began unpacking the picnic bag.

"You sound so self-sufficient," Michelle said, flashing him a sexy smile. She winked. "You do realize, don't you, that life is better when you share it with other people?"

"You mean, with a family?" Nick arranged paper plates, plastic cups and bowls on the table with geometric precision.

Michelle squealed like a teenage girl. "Yes!"

Nick wanted to tell Michelle that he had just begun his career. He wanted to say that he was not ready to support a family. But he would rather wait for the right moment. He smiled at her. "Thanks for telling me about your children."

"I hope it didn't upset you." She held out her cup.

Nick filled it and then his own. "Why would it?"

She lowered her head.

"How old are your kids?" Nick asked, gazing around the lush green lawn. The day had turned warm, and the shade offered cool respite.

Michelle cleared her throat. "The girls are three. They're twins. And my son just turned five."

"They must be a handful!"

"Children are a blessing," she said defiantly.

Nick swallowed a mouthful of chicken and washed it down with a mouthful of wine. "Do they look like their father?"

Michelle looked away for a moment. A pair of female joggers ran past their table and Nick could see the sweat staining their tight T-shirts. He couldn't take his eyes off their bouncing buttocks. He realized Michelle was speaking again.

"They look like me and their fathers." She was glowing with pride.

Nick wondered about the fathers of Michelle's children. Were they in regular contact with her and her children? "How did it end with your children's fathers?" Nick took another bite of chicken and fixed Michelle with a cool stare.

Michelle remained silent for a moment. Then she looked into Nick's eyes and said, "I told you. I was unlucky."

"What happened?"

"They were just idiots. They ran away because they didn't have the guts to take responsibility for us. It's hard to find a real man."

"So they just left you alone with the kids?"

Michelle took a slug of wine. "The first guy got me pregnant, and then he lost his job and couldn't find anything new. He was totally useless. I didn't want to stay with him. I figured if he couldn't support us, I'd be better off without him. I figured I could find a better man." She took a deep breath. "He said he'd send us some money as soon as he found a job, but I never heard from him again. What a loser." Michelle shook her head and scowled.

"Ah, so money is the most important criteria for you," Nick said, raising his eyebrows.

"I have three children. I need to be with a man who earns a fair amount of money."

Nick looked down into his cup. He could see what Michelle was all about. He tried to hide his disappointment. "How long had you been together?"

"Six months."

"Don't you think it would have been smart to wait a little longer before you started a family? What about the other guy?"

Michelle's face flushed. "I didn't tell him about my son right away."

"Sounds familiar."

"When I finally told him, he said it was fine. Then he got me pregnant with the twins. So suddenly we had three kids. He got scared and I could tell he wanted to leave." Michelle appeared close to tears.

Nick remained unmoved by her display of emotion. He remembered that one of the men in the YouTube clips had talked about women crying to get their way. "So what did you do?"

"I did everything within my power to make him stay." Michelle ran a hand through her hair. "One day, he said he'd found a position in New York City, but that it would be too expensive to move there with the whole family, so he wanted to go alone. I told him that if he abandoned me, I would kill myself."

Nick started to break out in a cold sweat. He felt light-headed. "Holy shit."

"I had three children, and I had just turned twenty-one. What the hell was I going to do if this asshole left me? A few days later, I went to visit my mom. When I came back, he was gone. I haven't seen him since. He doesn't send any money, either. Gone. Fucking asshole."

"But don't you accept that it was partly your fault?"

Michelle's nostrils flared. "*My* fault? He was a scared little bitch. Just like the first guy."

Nick's body tensed. He didn't know what to say. A wave of anger, anxiety and pity washed over him. He gazed at the greenery and remained silent for a long time. Right then, he knew it was over between them. He would not allow her to enslave him. These were her problems, not his.

Michelle cocked her head. "Don't you want to have children?" It sounded more like a command than a question.

A cold silence enveloped them. As Michelle drained her cup of wine, Nick found himself computing the cost of each child in his head. But it wasn't just the money. He was only twenty-five. He was still building his career. There were so many things he hadn't done yet. He might be able to handle one child, but three? Four? He didn't feel ready to start a family, let alone caring for three children he hadn't brought into the world.

Nick took a deep breath. "Honestly, I don't think we should see each other again."

Michelle's brow furrowed. Anger flashed in her eyes. "*What?*"

"I think you've made enough bad choices already. I'm not going to make another one with you."

"I love my children! I wouldn't have it any other way."

Nick began to feel sorry for Michelle. He reminded himself to stay strong. "Isn't life stressful enough with three kids?"

"Well, sure, but my mother helps me out."

Nick gasped. "You live with your mom?"

"Yes." Her expression was stoic.

Nick stabbed his fork into the potato salad. "How convenient."

"It is," Michelle said, oblivious to his sarcastic tone. "We get along really well. She helps me out with the kids so I can work part-time."

"Part-time? So you don't have medical insurance?"

"We're on my mother's insurance."

"Are you aware that it costs approximately three hundred grand to raise a child from birth until the age of eighteen? How are you planning to put your kids through college?"

"By that time, I'll probably be married."

Nick felt the hair on his neck bristle. "Good luck with that. I wouldn't marry you, but I'm sure you'll find some schmuck who will."

Her face turned white. "Don't you think it's about time you grew up? Life isn't always going to be about you, Nick."

"Damn it, Michelle! I'm twenty-five. I'm not even thinking about marriage or children at this point."

Michelle's eyes widened. "So you were just using me?"

"Honey, let's be real. Who's using whom?"

She reached out and stroked the back of his hand. "Don't you want to experience the joy of fatherhood?"

Nick recoiled from her touch. "I'm not their father! They're someone else's kids. They would never love or respect me."

"You're just like my exes!" She blinked away tears. "I feel so used."

"*You* feel used? How the hell do you think *I* feel? You should have been honest with me from the start."

"I love you!" Michelle scrubbed her eyes and smiled as if she had life completely figured out.

"I'm not interested in that kind of love." Nick gathered their trash and tucked it into a plastic sack. An eerie silence descended upon them. They looked at each other as if they had never previously met.

"I once thought you were a beautiful woman. But you're a liar. And liars are ugly."

Her eyes began to fill with tears.

Nick felt enraged and more powerful than ever. "I'm looking forward to jacking off to porn on my new eighty-inch TV. It'll be a thousand times more real than fucking you," Nick said quietly and walked away.

Meeting Michelle had a lasting impact on Nick's perspective on dating, women and life in general. And Nick was grateful for the transformation. He credited his newfound insight and empowerment to the men of the MGTOW movement. There are millions of single moms prowling the Internet in search of security for their babies. Every day, thousands of men are lured by the promise of love and sex into a life of enslavement. The man who marries a single mother will never be number one in her life. Her children will always come first. His role will be that of the provider. His value is the worth of his bank account.

Hook-up apps and dating websites are where opportunists, gold-diggers and scam artists hunt their prey, luring them in with sex and affection. Nick decided that there was a huge difference between online profiles and the people who hid behind them. He deleted all his profiles and apps. Instead, he focused on getting to know the real people around him. Nick was surprised at how popular he became. People liked him for his unique attributes, and not because they considered him to be a source of financial security. Before long, he was promoted at work. His new position involved traveling to technology events around the world.

When friends visited Philadelphia, Nick would take them on tours of the city. At the Liberty Bell, he'd recount the story of how he had almost become enslaved to a woman and her three children. At the age of twenty-seven, he found that single life provided everything he could possibly want. He still invested his time and money in the pursuit of women, but he also developed shared interests with friends. Nick loved his career and he loved to socialize. Every year, he would take a large group of friends to see the Phillies play and treat them to hot dogs and beer. He arranged annual trips to Las Vegas where he and his friends would let their hair down and do all of the things that happen in Vegas and are best left there.

IBM paid him quarterly stock options. Nick began to play the stock market, achieving moderate but consistent success. It didn't take long before he turned his attention to long-term investments in mutual funds. He became comfortably well-off, and for a while he toyed with the idea of buying fancy cars and other luxury goods. But then he thought about the kind of woman such an image would attract and decided instead to stick with public transport and a cardio-inducing bike. Nick didn't want to invite that kind of woman into his life. At least, not for longer than a night.

Whenever Nick flashed back to his encounter with Michelle, he remembered clearly her insecurity and the deep-seated fear of poverty that led her to prostitute her body and her emotions. He vowed that he would never entertain a relationship that was heavily based upon any kind of fiscal strategy. After his relationship with Michelle had forced him to question his attitude towards being single, he realized he wasn't all that eager to enter a romantic liaison. He was twenty-seven. He should be out there playing the field rather than allowing himself to be pinned down by one woman's wants and needs.

## Nickolas Stern's Lessons Learned

1. It's easy to hide behind a dating profile. The medium lends itself to dishonesty. Profiles can be manipulated, and pictures can be airbrushed. No level of frequency or intensity of messaging can reveal a person's true character. Not all women are opportunists or gold-diggers, but women with children from previous relationships will prioritize financial security in order to provide for their families.

2. Sex evokes many potent emotions, and it's easy to fall in lust and to mistake that for falling in love. Once that happens, it's difficult to make sensible decisions.

3. By cutting off the sexual element of the relationship, one can find the presence of mind to weigh up the consequences of committing to a lifelong obligation and its accompanying investment and return.

4. On average, it costs $300,000 in America to raise a child from birth until the age of eighteen. This is equivalent to the price of a house, and doesn't even include the cost of a college education.

5. Holding onto income and investing improves self-esteem.

6. Attending workshops or gatherings, joining clubs or societies and engaging any study- or work-related activities puts you in contact with people who share your interests. Meeting in the real world provides the best way to establish relationships built on openness and honesty.

The epilogue is the author's sign off.

# Epilogue

People have asked me why I'm so passionate about the men's liberation movement. There are many reasons, but I suppose my critical lens was shaped early on. I watched as my personal hero, my father, slaved long hours and weekends to feed and clothe siblings, my mother and me. He toiled in rain, mud, ice and snow and never took a day off, even when he was suffering from work-related injuries. Unfortunately, that meant he never lived his own dreams; he suffered the exasperation and frustration of being enslaved as the family's sole provider. I gifted my father and mother first-class tickets and lodging to anywhere in the world. They chose to visit me. When he passed away after decades of hard labor, his body battered and his face sun-dried like a raisin, I could see that his unempowered life had taken a big toll.

Over and over again, I've witnessed similar developments in the families of individuals I've met or become friends with. Throughout my life, I've seen men who have been involuntarily consigned to the role of workhorse--and little else. I planned my escape from that fate in my early years. I've lived the life my father never had. I traveled the world, made good money, invested, built things and enjoyed pursuing my dreams. My life has been a carousel ride jam-packed with freedom, love and success; I've learned many things, especially about those things *that bring* true happiness. Needless to say, having sufficient resources has allowed me to nourish my curiosity, embrace other cultures and meet amazing people. I wish all of you might experience such a fate.

Remember, the best is yet to come.

Tim Patten

i     http://gynocentrism.com/

ii     http://www.theguardian.com/money/2014/feb/11/millennials-feel-high-cost-dating-valentine

iii     https://dontmarry.wordpress.com/

iv     http://legacy.fordham.edu/campus_resources/enewsroom/archives/archive_2501.asp

v     http://www.familyshare.com/parenting/mens-roles-in-a-family-as-provider-and-protector-honoring-and-serving-your-family

vi     http://money.cnn.com/2015/03/12/pf/planning-for-wedding-costs/

vii     http://money.cnn.com/2014/08/18/pf/child-cost/

viii     http://www.huffingtonpost.com/2014/08/18/cost-of-raising-a-child_n_5688179.html

ix     http://www.mgtow.com/shaming-tactics/

x     http://ncfm.org/2014/11/news/discrimination-news/against-men-news/ncfm-supporter-timothy-patten-are-men-winning-the-battle-of-the-sexes/

xi     https://www.psychologytoday.com/blog/owning-pink/201408/women-please-stop-shaming-men

xii     http://www.slate.com/articles/news_and_politics/foreigners/2009/06/the_herbivores_dilemma.html

xiii     https://rmaxgenactivepua.wordpress.com/2013/07/02/the-marriage-strike-hitting-women-hard/

xiv     http://www.dailymail.co.uk/health/article-2623873/You-really-nagged-death-Excessive-demands-partners-double-risk-dying-middle-age.html

xv     http://www.dailymail.co.uk/health/article-2623873/You-really-nagged-death-Excessive-demands-partners-double-risk-dying-middle-age.html

xvi     http://www.dailymail.co.uk/health/article-2623873/You-really-nagged-death-Excessive-demands-partners-double-risk-dying-middle-age.html

xvii     https://broadly.vice.com/en_us/video/the-land-of-no-men-inside-kenyas-women-only-village

xviii     http://www.jjmccullough.com/charts_rest_female-leaders.php

xix     http://www.cawp.rutgers.edu/current-numbers

xx     http://www.dol.gov/wb/factsheets/Qf-laborforce-10.htm

xxi     https://www.nwbc.gov/facts/new-fact-sheet-women-owned-businesses

xxii

xxiii

xxiv     https://en.wikipedia.org/wiki/Gregory_Goodwin_Pincus

Printed in the United States
By Bookmasters